YOUR recipe could appear in our next cookbook!

Share your tried & true family favorites with us instantly at

www.gooseberrypatch.com

If you'd rather jot 'em down by hand, just mail this form to...

Gooseberry Patch • Cookbooks – Call for Recipes
PO Box 812 • Columbus, OH 43216-0812

If your recipe is selected for a book, you'll receive a FREE copy!

Please share only your original recipes or those that you have made your own over the years.

Recipe Name:

Number of Servings:

Any fond memories about this recipe? Special touches you like to add
or handy shortcuts?

Ingredients (include specific measurements):

Instructions (continue on back if needed):

Special Code: **cookbookspage**

Over ↗

Extra space for recipe if needed:

Tell us about yourself...

Your complete contact information is needed so that we can send you your FREE cookbook, if your recipe is published. Phone numbers and email addresses are kept private and will only be used if we have questions about your recipe.

Name:

Address:

City: State: Zip:

Email:

Daytime Phone:

Thank you! Vickie & Jo Ann

Gooseberry Patch

An imprint of Globe Pequot
246 Goose Lane
Guilford, CT 06437

www.gooseberrypatch.com

1•800•854•6673

Copyright 2014, Gooseberry Patch   978-1-62093-171-4

Do you have a tried & true recipe...

tip, craft or memory that you'd like to see featured in
a **Gooseberry Patch** cookbook? Visit our website at
www.gooseberrypatch.com, register and follow the
easy steps to submit your favorite family recipe.
Or send them to us at:

Gooseberry Patch
PO Box 812
Columbus, OH 43216-0812

Don't forget to include the number of servings your recipe makes,
plus your name, address, phone number and email address. If we
select your recipe, your name will appear right along with it...
and you'll receive a **FREE** copy of the book!

Contents

Dedication

To busy moms who want to spend more time with family this fall and less time in the kitchen.

Appreciation

A big thanks to everyone who shared their can't-miss recipes for the season with us.

Breakfast
ON THE GO

Oven Omelet Brunch

Gladys Kielar
Whitehouse, OH

Breakfast for a bunch is so fast and easy with this recipe! Add a basket of muffins and brunch is served. If you aren't feeding a crowd, it's simple to cut the recipe in half.

1/4 c. butter, sliced
1-1/2 doz. eggs
1 c. milk
1 c. sour cream

1 t. salt
1 c. shredded Cheddar cheese
1/4 c. green onions, chopped

Place butter in a 13"x9" baking pan. Melt in a 325-degree oven, tilting pan to cover bottom completely; set aside. In a large bowl, beat eggs, milk, sour cream and salt until blended. Stir in cheese and onions; pour into baking pan. Bake, uncovered, at 325 degrees until eggs are set, about 30 to 35 minutes. Cut into squares. Makes 10 to 12 servings.

The first day back to school usually means a busy morning, so why not make a simple overnight breakfast dish? Putting it together the night before means less fuss in the morning and the kids get off to a great start.

Breakfast ON THE GO

Hanna's Favorite French Toast

Hanna Donner
Grandview, MO

My mother taught me this recipe when I was young...I still love it!

2 eggs, beaten
2 T. milk
1/2 c. sugar
1 t. cinnamon
1 t. vanilla extract

1 T. butter, divided
4 slices honey wheat bread
Garnish: creamy peanut butter,
    maple syrup, powdered sugar

In a shallow dish, beat eggs with milk, sugar, cinnamon and vanilla; set aside. Melt half of butter in a skillet over medium heat. Dip 2 bread slices in egg mixture, coating well on both sides; add to skillet. Cook for about 2 minutes, until golden; turn and cook other side. Repeat with remaining butter and bread. Serve slices topped with peanut butter and maple syrup; sprinkle with powdered sugar. Makes 4 servings.

French toast can be frozen, how handy! Make French toast the usual way and cool completely. Layer slices with wax paper and place in a plastic freezer bag. To serve, simply pop a slice in the toaster until crisp.

Bubble Breakfast Pizza

Linda Kilgore
Kittanning, PA

A quick, delicious breakfast that's a family favorite! Try it with crisp bacon instead of sausage too.

16-oz. pkg. ground pork
   breakfast sausage
1 doz. eggs
1/2 c. milk
1 T. butter

16-oz. tube refrigerated jumbo
   biscuits
8-oz. pkg. pasteurized process
   cheese spread, sliced

Brown sausage in a large skillet over medium heat; drain and set aside. Whisk together eggs and milk in a large bowl. Wipe out skillet; melt butter over low heat and add egg mixture. Cook and stir until eggs are lightly scrambled. While eggs are cooking, separate biscuits and press into a greased 13"x9" baking pan, forming a crust. Spoon scrambled eggs over biscuits; top with sausage and cheese. Bake, uncovered, at 375 degrees for 30 minutes, or until biscuits are set and cheese melts. Serves 8.

Many farmers' markets are open well into autumn. Visit a nearby market for just-harvested fruits & vegetables, eggs, baked goods, jams & jellies...perfect for farm-fresh breakfasts.

Mama Meg's Breakfast Biscuits

Megan Kreplin
Coxsackie, NY

My sons are big breakfast fans. The first time I made these, the boys took a taste and their eyes really lit up. It's so handy to keep the biscuits frozen for a quick breakfast on the way out.

8-oz. tube refrigerated biscuits
4 eggs, beaten
1 T. milk
salt and pepper to taste

2 t. butter
8 slices American cheese
8 thin slices cooked deli ham or
   crisply cooked bacon

Bake biscuits according to package directions; cool for 5 minutes. Meanwhile, in a bowl, whisk together eggs, milk and seasonings. Melt butter in a skillet over medium heat. Add egg mixture; scramble to desired doneness. Top eggs with cheese; let stand until melted, then slice eggs into 8 equal pieces. Split biscuits. Top each biscuit bottom with egg, ham or bacon and biscuit top. Serve immediately. To freeze, wrap each biscuit in plastic wrap. Place all biscuits in a plastic zipping bag and freeze. To serve, remove from freezer and microwave for 45 seconds. Makes 8 servings.

Fall conjures up so many memories! September reminds me of new school clothes and freshly sharpened pencils. It's time to make the house cozy, warm and inviting. I love everything about October. It is the month my daughter Keli was born and I can sense that a change is coming...it's time for pumpkins and gourds, Indian corn and sunflowers. On a crisp day when the colors of autumn are at their peak, I visit my favorite cider mill and bring home a jug of fresh cider just off the apple presses and an abundance of pumpkin doughnuts. My favorite time of year!

–Sherry Svoboda, Bel Air, MD

Apple Ring Pancakes

Becky Drees
Pittsfield, MA

You just have to try these! They're like a scrumptious cross between pancakes, apple pie and fried dough.

1 c. biscuit baking mix
1/2 c. milk
1 egg, beaten
1 t. pumpkin pie spice

zest of 1/2 lemon
2 apples, peeled
Garnish: pancake syrup

Combine biscuit mix, milk, egg, spice and zest in a bowl. Stir until blended; set aside. Cut apples horizontally into 1/8-inch slices, coring out the centers to make rings. Dip apple rings into batter; add to a greased griddle over medium heat. Cook on both sides until golden. Serve with syrup. Serves 2.

Pumpkin Pancakes

Cris Goode
Mooresville, IN

When I make these pancakes with my daughter, we use cookie cutters to cut them into fun shapes! Serve with butter and syrup, or try cream cheese or pumpkin dip for a special treat.

2 c. biscuit baking mix
1/2 c. canned pumpkin
1 c. water

1 egg white, beaten
2 t. pumpkin pie spice
Garnish: butter, pancake syrup

Combine all ingredients except garnish in a bowl; beat well. Pour batter onto a greased griddle by 1/4 cupfuls. Cook over medium heat until golden on both sides. Serve with butter and syrup. Makes 6 servings.

Take your family's breakfast outdoors! Spread a quilt on the picnic table and enjoy the cool morning air.

Breakfast
ON THE GO

Oven Pancake

Paulette Alexander
Saint George's, Newfoundland

I love being able to bake this pancake in the oven. It frees up the stovetop to cook breakfast bacon or ham at the same time.

3 eggs, beaten
1/2 c. milk
1/2 c. all-purpose flour

1/4 t. salt
1 T. butter, melted
Garnish: pancake syrup

In a bowl, whisk together eggs, milk, flour and salt until smooth. Spread butter in a 9" pie plate; add batter. Bake at 400 degrees for about 20 minutes, until cooked through. Serve with pancake syrup. Serves 4.

Cinnamon-Maple Apples

Andrea Heyart
Savannah, TX

Delicious as a pancake topping or as a side dish for sausages or pork chops. A family favorite for sure!

2 T. butter
3 to 4 apples, peeled, cored and
    sliced into wedges
1/4 c. maple syrup

1/4 c. brown sugar, packed
1 t. cinnamon
1/4 t. nutmeg

In a skillet over medium heat, melt butter and add sliced apples. Toss to coat; simmer until apples begin to soften. Add remaining ingredients to skillet. Simmer over medium heat, stirring often, until sauce is thickened and bubbly. Serves 4.

Fresh eggs can safely be kept in the refrigerator for four to five weeks...go ahead and stock up when they're on sale.

Snookie's Coffee Cake

Julie Wiesen
Houston, TX

I have made this coffee cake at least 75 times over the past six years for my children and their friends, sports teams and teachers. It is crazy how it has become such a hit with my kids and their school!

2/3 c. brown sugar, packed
4 t. cinnamon
18-1/2 oz. pkg. butter golden
   cake mix

4 eggs, beaten
2/3 c. oil
1 c. buttermilk
1/4 c. sugar

Mix brown sugar and cinnamon in a cup; set aside. In a large bowl, combine dry cake mix and remaining ingredients. Beat for 3 to 4 minutes with an electric mixer on medium speed. Pour half of batter into a greased 13"x9" baking pan; sprinkle with half of brown sugar mixture. Repeat layers; swirl through both layers with a table knife. Bake at 325 degrees for 40 minutes, or until set. Remove pan to a wire rack, being very careful not to shake the pan, as the cake will sink in the center if you do. Drizzle Powdered Sugar Icing over cooled cake; cut into squares. Makes 10 to 12 servings.

Powdered Sugar Icing:

1 to 1-1/2 c. powdered sugar
1 to 2 T. milk, divided

1 t. vanilla extract

Beat together powdered sugar and one tablespoon milk. Beat in more milk as needed for a drizzling consistency. Stir in vanilla.

Drizzle a frosting glaze over breakfast treats in a jiffy. Spoon glaze into a plastic zipping bag, snip off a tiny corner and drizzle away. Then just toss away the bag... couldn't be simpler!

Butterscotch Bubbles

Joyce Keeling
Springfield, MO

I received this recipe from a pen pal when I was just ten years old. It was the first recipe that I made by myself, and I was thrilled that my family liked it so much. Whenever company arrived, Mom would tell me, "Go make some of your bubbles." I was so proud when I served them... after just one taste, they'd ask for my recipe!

1/4 c. butter, melted
1/4 c. brown sugar, packed
1/4 c. chopped nuts

1/2 t. cinnamon
8-oz. tube refrigerated biscuits, quartered

Place melted butter in a shallow dish; set aside. In a shallow dish, mix together brown sugar, nuts and cinnamon. Dip biscuit pieces into butter, then into brown sugar mixture. Arrange biscuits on ungreased baking sheets. Bake at 475 degrees for 10 minutes, or until lightly golden. Serve warm. Makes about 3-1/2 dozen pieces.

A mini photo album is just right for keeping go-to recipes handy on the kitchen counter. Tuck in a few photos of happy family mealtimes too!

Banana-Oat Breakfast Cookies
Sandra Sullivan
Aurora, CO

*Need something new for breakfast? These satisfying cookies are
great with a glass of cold milk or a cup of hot coffee.*

1/2 c. ripe banana, mashed
1/2 c. crunchy peanut butter
1/2 c. honey
1 t. vanilla extract
1 c. quick-cooking oats,
   uncooked

1/2 c. whole-wheat flour
1/4 c. powdered milk
2 t. cinnamon
1/4 t. baking soda
1 c. sweetened dried cranberries
   or raisins

In a large bowl, stir together banana, peanut butter, honey and
vanilla; set aside. In a small bowl, combine oats, flour, powdered milk,
cinnamon and baking soda. Add oat mixture to banana mixture; stir
until blended. Fold in cranberries or raisins. Lightly coat 2 baking
sheets with non-stick vegetable spray. Drop mounds of dough onto
baking sheets by 1/4 cupfuls, 3 inches apart. With a spatula dipped in
water, flatten each mound into a 2-3/4 inch circle, about 1/2-inch
thick. Bake at 350 degrees, one sheet at a time, for 14 to 16 minutes,
until golden. Transfer cookies to wire racks to cool. Store in an airtight
container up to 3 days. Cookies may also be cooled, wrapped and
frozen; thaw before serving. Makes one dozen.

Egg dishes are a terrific way to use up tasty tidbits from
the fridge...chopped veggies, deli meats and cheese. Warm
ingredients briefly in the skillet before scrambling in the eggs.

Chocolate-Peanut Butter Granola Bars

Amy Bradsher
Roxboro, NC

We keep these sweet & satisfying bars stashed in the fridge for on-the-go breakfasts and quick snacks. My kids love to try to sneak a taste as they help me mix them up!

2 c. quick-cooking oats, uncooked
1/2 c. sunflower seed kernels
1/2 c. unsweetened flaked coconut

1/2 c. semi-sweet chocolate chips
1/2 c. peanuts, coarsely chopped
2/3 c. creamy peanut butter
1/3 c. honey

In a bowl, mix together all ingredients except peanut butter and honey; set aside. In a small saucepan over low heat, melt peanut butter and honey together; stir until blended. Pour peanut butter mixture over oat mixture; stir until combined and mixture is sticky. If mixture is too dry, drizzle in a little bit more honey and mix well. Press into a greased 8"x8" baking pan. Bake at 225 degrees for 20 to 30 minutes; cool slightly. Cut into bars and wrap individually. For firmer bars, keep refrigerated. Makes one dozen.

A little coffee brings out the flavor in any chocolate recipe. Just dissolve a tablespoon of instant coffee granules in liquid ingredients and continue as directed.

Amy's Biscuit, Egg & Gravy Casserole

Amy Snyder
Beckley, WV

I like this hearty casserole any time of the year, but it's a true comfort meal to get a chilly day started right. It warms tummies and your family time warms your heart.

16-oz. pkg. ground pork
   breakfast sausage
16-oz. tube refrigerated jumbo
   biscuits
1 c. shredded Cheddar cheese

6 eggs, beaten
1/2 c. milk
salt and pepper to taste
1-1/2 oz. pkg. country
   gravy mix

Brown sausage in a skillet over medium heat; drain. Spray a 13"x9" baking pan with non-stick vegetable spray; set aside. Separate biscuits and tear into one-inch pieces; line the bottom of pan with biscuit pieces. Scatter browned sausage over biscuits; sprinkle sausage with cheese. Whisk together eggs, milk and seasonings; pour over cheese. Prepare gravy mix according to package directions; spoon over egg mixture. Bake, uncovered, at 350 degrees for 30 to 40 minutes, checking after 30 minutes, until firm in the center. Makes 6 to 8 servings.

Start a tailgating Saturday right...invite friends to join you for breakfast. Keep it simple with a breakfast casserole, baskets of sweet rolls and a fresh fruit salad. It's all about food and friends!

● *Breakfast* ●
ON THE GO

Ham, Egg & Cheesewich

Wendy Jo Minotte
Duluth, MN

I taught my children how to make this quick and tasty breakfast sandwich. Enjoy with a glass of orange juice.

2 slices bread, toasted
3 t. butter, softened and divided
1 egg
1 slice American cheese

salt to taste
3 to 4 thin slices cooked
    deli ham

Spread each slice of toast with one teaspoon butter; set aside. Melt remaining butter in a skillet over medium-low heat. Crack egg into skillet; break yolk with a fork or leave whole. Cook until egg is nearly set; turn over with a spatula. Season with salt; top with cheese and remove to a plate. Add stacked ham to skillet; warm on both sides. Top ham with egg and cheese; sandwich ham and egg stack between toast slices. Makes one serving.

Breakfast Burritos

Lauren Vanden Berg
Grandville, MI

I make these breakfast treats all the time...it only takes 15 to 20 minutes to make a stack of them.

1 lb. ground pork breakfast
    sausage
1 green pepper, diced

8 eggs, beaten
1 c. shredded Cheddar cheese
8 burrito-size flour tortillas

Brown sausage with green pepper in a skillet over medium heat; drain. Add eggs and cheese to skillet; cook and stir until eggs are set. Divide mixture among tortillas; fold tortillas burrito-style. Makes 8 servings.

Paper coffee filters make tidy holders for breakfast burritos... easy for little hands to hold too.

Blueberry Cheese Danish

JoAnna Nicoline-Haughey
Berwyn, PA

I make this special treat for my daughter's teachers.
The school staff loves it...it's so simple but tastes like I have been
baking all morning! Try it with cherry pie filling too.

2 8-oz. tubes refrigerated
  crescent rolls
2 8-oz. pkgs. cream cheese,
  softened
1 egg, separated

3/4 c. sugar
1 t. vanilla extract
21-oz. can blueberry pie filling
Garnish: cinnamon-sugar

Lightly grease a 13"x9" baking pan. Unroll one tube of crescent rolls and place in bottom of pan; set aside. In a bowl, blend cream cheese, egg yolk, sugar and vanilla; spread over crescent rolls. Spoon pie filling over cream cheese mixture. Unroll remaining crescent rolls and place on top. Whisk egg white in a cup until foamy; spread over crescents. Sprinkle with cinnamon-sugar. Bake at 350 degrees for 25 to 30 minutes. Cool completely; cut into squares. Makes 10 to 12 servings.

Turn old wool sweaters into a stack of cozy felt mug coasters. Just wash sweaters in very hot water, then place them in the dryer set to hot. When dry, cut out circles or squares. Decorate the edges with colorful yarn in a simple whip stitch.

Berry Yummy French Toast

Sue Klapper
Muskego, WI

Start your day deliciously!

2 slices bread, cut one-inch
   thick
3 T. strawberry preserves
1 T. chopped pecans
1 egg, lightly beaten
1/3 c. milk

1-1/2 t. sugar
1/4 t. vanilla extract
2 T. butter, softened
2 T. powdered sugar, divided
1/4 c. strawberries, hulled
   and sliced

Cut a pocket in one end of each bread slice, cutting almost but not quite through to the other end. In a small bowl, mix strawberry preserves and pecans. Stuff half of the mixture into the pocket in each slice. In a pie plate, whisk together egg, milk, sugar and vanilla. Melt butter on a griddle over medium-high heat. Carefully dip bread slices into egg mixture on both sides. Cook on griddle until golden on one side; turn and sprinkle half of the powdered sugar over both slices. Cook until golden on other side. Turn again and sprinkle with remaining powdered sugar. Serve topped with strawberries. Makes 2 servings.

Stir up a super-simple fruit topping for pancakes and waffles. Combine a can of fruit pie filling and 2 tablespoons orange juice in a small bowl. Microwave for 2 to 2-1/2 minutes, stirring twice. Serve warm.

19

Cowboy Breakfast Casserole

Sandy Perry
Bakersfield, CA

This is an easy crowd-pleaser! It's a great way to use up leftover baked potatoes...don't be tempted to use frozen potatoes in this recipe. My whole family loves this one and they request it often.

1 doz. eggs, lightly beaten
2-1/2 c. shredded Cheddar
   cheese, divided
1 c. whipping cream
1 green pepper, chopped
1/2 c. onion, chopped

2 baked potatoes, peeled
   and chopped
salt and pepper to taste
1 lb. bacon, ground pork
   sausage or ham, cooked
Garnish: sour cream, salsa

Pour eggs into a greased 13"x9" baking pan. Sprinkle with one cup cheese; pour cream over top. Layer with remaining ingredients except garnish, ending with remaining cheese. Do not stir. Bake, uncovered, at 350 degrees for 50 to 60 minutes. Let stand for 5 minutes; cut into squares. Serve topped with sour cream and salsa. Makes 8 to 10 servings.

Whip up some special hot cocoa with a round disc of Mexican chocolate...the sugar and cinnamon are already mixed in. Bring 4 cups milk almost to a boil, add the chopped chocolate and whisk until it's melted and creamy.

Breakfast ON THE GO

Citrus-Glazed Fruit Salad

Pamela Myers
Auburn, IN

This fruit salad is the absolute best! I can't tell you how many times I've been asked for the recipe. I serve it with sweet rolls for breakfast and with cake for dessert. The glaze prevents the fruit from turning brown, so it keeps well for a few days in the refrigerator. Change up the fruit to suit your family's taste...I've also used apples and kiwi.

4 c. strawberries, hulled
   and sliced
4 c. blueberries
2 c. seedless green grapes,
   halved
2 to 3 ripe bananas, sliced
11-oz. can mandarin oranges,
   drained

20-oz. can pineapple tidbits,
   drained and juice reserved
1/3 c. orange juice
1 T. lemon juice
1/2 c. sugar
2 T. cornstarch

In a serving bowl, combine all of the fruit; set aside. In a saucepan, combine reserved pineapple juice, orange juice, lemon juice, sugar and cornstarch. Cook and stir over medium heat until thickened and bubbly. Remove from heat; set aside. Pour warm sauce over fruit and stir gently to coat. Cover and refrigerate. Makes 12 to 16 servings.

Serve pancakes with cheery pumpkin faces! Cut an apple into thin slices, then cut triangles for the eyes and nose. Give Jack a happy smile with an apple slice for his mouth.

Angie's Easy Pancakes

Evangeline Boston
Bradenton, FL

I have been using this recipe for more than 30 years and my kids grew up on them. It's easy, no-fail and tastes so good, even plain. There's no need to buy pancake mix...you have it all in your pantry!

2 c. all-purpose flour
1/2 c. sugar
4-1/2 t. baking powder
1 t. salt
2 eggs, beaten
2 c. milk

1/4 c. butter, melted and slightly cooled
Optional: 1/2 c. blueberries, chocolate chips or chopped pecans
Garnish: butter, pancake syrup

In a large bowl, combine flour, sugar, baking powder and salt; mix well and set aside. In a separate bowl, whisk together eggs, milk and melted butter. Add egg mixture to flour mixture; stir until all big lumps are gone. Stir in optional ingredients, if desired. Spoon batter onto a greased hot griddle by 1/4 cupfuls. Cook until golden on both sides. Serve topped with butter and syrup. Leftover pancakes freeze well. Makes 12 to 15, 5-inch pancakes.

Apple Cider Syrup

Samantha Starks
Madison, WI

This yummy syrup is delicious over waffles, pancakes or any kind of apple dessert.

1/2 c. sugar
4 t. cornstarch
1 t. cinnamon

1 c. apple cider or apple juice
1 T. lemon juice
2 T. butter, sliced

In a small saucepan, combine sugar, cornstarch and cinnamon. Stir in apple cider or juice and lemon juice. Cook over medium heat, stirring constantly, until thickened and bubbly. Cook and stir an additional 2 minutes. Remove from heat; stir in butter. Serve hot. Makes about 1-1/2 cups.

Autumn Amish Baked Oatmeal

Karen Sampson
Waymart, PA

My grandkids Silas and Eliza have enjoyed this tasty fall breakfast treat since they were toddlers. Especially when we top it with a splash of Grandpa's homemade maple syrup!

Optional: 1/2 c. diced apples,
   1/2 c. raisins
1-1/2 c. long-cooking oats,
   uncooked
1/2 c. brown sugar, packed
1 egg, beaten

1/4 c. oil
1 c. milk
1 t. baking powder
1 t. cinnamon
Garnish: additional milk

Layer apples and/or raisins in the bottom of a greased 9"x9" baking pan, if using; set aside. Beat together remaining ingredients except garnish with a spoon. Pour oat mixture into pan. Bake, uncovered, at 300 degrees for 30 to 35 minutes. Serve topped with milk. Serves 6.

Quick Oats for One

Wendy Jo Minotte
Duluth, MN

This makes very fluffy oatmeal for a quick, healthy breakfast, and almost no clean-up afterwards.

1 c. quick-cooking oats,
   uncooked
1-1/2 c. boiling water

Garnish: milk, sugar, cinnamon,
   dried fruit

Place oats in a heat-proof cereal bowl. Pour boiling water over oats; water should just cover oats. Cover the bowl with a plate and let stand for 5 minutes. Garnish as desired. Makes one serving.

Hang an old-fashioned peg rack inside the back door...you'll always know where to find your scarf, the kids' backpacks and the dog's leash!

Sweet Bacon Monkey Bread

Polly McCallum
Palatka, FL

A new take on monkey bread that everyone is sure to love!

6 slices bacon
2 T. butter
2 T. maple syrup
1/4 c. brown sugar, packed

1/4 t. cinnamon
2 8-oz. tubes refrigerated
   crescent dinner rolls

In a skillet over medium heat, cook bacon until crisp; drain on paper towels. Combine butter and syrup in a microwave-safe bowl. Microwave on high, uncovered, for 30 to 45 seconds, until hot. Add brown sugar and cinnamon; stir until dissolved. Spray an 8"x4" loaf pan with non-stick vegetable spray; gently pour butter mixture into pan. Crumble bacon over top. Unroll one tube of rolls into a large rectangle; press perforations to seal. Cut rectangle into 8 rows by 3 rows, to make 24 pieces. Repeat with remaining tube. Form each piece of dough into a ball; layer balls in pan. Bake at 350 degrees for 30 to 35 minutes, until golden. Cool in pan 5 minutes. Place a serving plate over pan; carefully turn out onto plate. Serve warm. Serves 8.

Greet guests with a harvest wreath on the front door. To a straw wreath, hot-glue sunflower heads and mini gourds. Tie on a big bow of homespun fabric and it's ready to display.

Whole-Wheat Pumpkin Bread

Julie Dossantos
Fort Pierce, FL

Toasted pumpkin bread with cream cheese is our breakfast tradition for Halloween and Thanksgiving. Also wonderful for a late-night snack!

3-1/2 c. whole-wheat flour	1 c. oil
3 c. sugar	15-oz. can pumpkin
2 t. baking soda	4 eggs, beaten
1-1/2 t. salt	2/3 c. water
2 t. cinnamon	1-1/2 t. vanilla extract
2 t. nutmeg	

Spray two 9"x5" loaf pans with non-stick vegetable spray; set aside. In a large bowl, combine flour, sugar, baking soda, salt and spices; mix well. Add oil, pumpkin, eggs, water and vanilla. Beat with an electric mixer on low speed until combined. Pour half of batter into each loaf pan. Bake at 350 degrees for 55 minutes to an hour, until loaves test done with a toothpick inserted in the center. Cool loaves in pans on a wire rack for 15 minutes; turn out of pans. Makes 2 loaves.

One of my favorite fall memories is of when my Uncle Kenny would hook up his small flatbed trailer to his lawn tractor for a ride in the woods. Grandma and Aunt Becky, who both had difficulty with walking and balance, would sit in old recliner chairs on the trailer and all the kids and other adults would huddle around them. By being so creative, my uncle made it possible for all of the family to enjoy the colors and scents of autumn. Afterwards we would have a bonfire snuggled under blankets and roasting marshmallows and hot dogs, and just enjoy talking and being together.

–Emily Edwards, Alliance, OH

Cinnamon Roll Breakfast Bake

Cheryl Culver
Perkins, OK

I like to have an easy tasty breakfast on weekends because I have so much to do. This breakfast bread pudding goes together in about ten minutes. I always gets requests for repeats...it's just so yummy!

4 eggs, beaten
1 c. plus 2 T. milk
2 T. sugar
1 t. vanilla extract

1/2 t. cinnamon
12 slices cinnamon raisin swirl
   bread, quartered

Spray a 9"x9" baking pan with cooking spray; set aside. In a large bowl, combine eggs, milk, sugar, vanilla and cinnamon; beat until smooth. Add bread pieces to bowl and stir into egg mixture, breaking bread into chunks, until liquid is absorbed. Let stand 5 minutes; transfer to baking pan. Bake at 350 degrees for 30 to 40 minutes, until puffed and a knife tip inserted near center tests clean. Spread Icing over warm casserole; cut into squares. Serves 9.

Icing:

2 c. powdered sugar
2 T. butter, softened

2 to 3 T. milk
1/4 t. vanilla extract

In a large bowl, combine powdered sugar, butter, 2 tablespoons milk and vanilla. Beat with an electric mixer on low speed until sugar is moistened. Increase to medium speed. Beat until smooth and spreadable, adding a little more milk if necessary.

I'm so glad I live in a world where there are Octobers.
–Lucy M. Montgomery

Melt-in-Your-Mouth
Pecan Rolls

Joyceann Dreibelbis
Wooster, OH

Your family will love these quickie sticky buns! They're easy to put together too...you'll be enjoying them in no time at all.

1/2 c. brown sugar, packed
1/2 c. butter, softened
1/4 c. corn syrup
2 8-oz. tubes refrigerated
   crescent dinner rolls

2/3 c. chopped pecans
1/4 c. sugar
1 t. cinnamon

In a small bowl, blend brown sugar, butter and corn syrup. Divide mixture between 2 greased 8"x8" baking pans; spread to coat bottoms and set aside. Unroll each tube of dough into a rectangle; press to seal perforations. Combine pecans, sugar, and cinnamon; sprinkle over dough. Separately roll up each rectangle, jelly-roll style, starting on one long side; seal edges. Cut each roll into 16 slices. Place slices cut-side down in pans. Bake at 375 degrees for 13 to 16 minutes, until golden. Cool in pans for one minute; turn rolls out onto serving plates Makes about 2-1/2 dozen.

Mismatched glass salt & pepper shakers make sweet mini vases for the breakfast table. Simply remove the tops, fill with water and tuck in a big blossom. Place one at each table setting for a colorful accent.

Bacon & Cheese Muffins

Tina Butler
Royse City, TX

*These savory breakfast muffins are perfect for on-the-go mornings
and busy school days. They can be frozen and reheated too.*

1/2 lb. bacon, diced
2 c. all-purpose flour
2 t. baking powder
1/4 t. salt
1/4 t. pepper

1-1/4 c. milk
1 egg, beaten
1/4 c. butter, melted and
   slightly cooled
3/4 c. shredded Cheddar cheese

In a skillet over medium heat, cook bacon until crisp; drain on paper
towels. Meanwhile, in a large bowl, stir together flour, baking powder,
salt and pepper. In a separate bowl, mix together milk, egg and melted
butter. Add milk mixture to flour mixture; stir just until moistened.
Fold in bacon and cheese just until combined. Fill greased or paper-
lined muffin cups 2/3 full. Bake at 400 degrees for 20 to 25 minutes,
until lightly golden. Serves 6.

Serve fuss-free favorites like Bacon & Cheese Muffins...
ideal for tailgating Saturday morning. Everyone can
easily help themselves while the day's fun is beginning.

Breakfast
ON THE GO

Nell's Sausage Muffins

Lynda Zickefoose
Lubbock, TX

*A dear friend in my Sunday School class shared this recipe with me.
I have made it my own by using a variety of meats like crumbled
bacon, diced ham and pepperoni...they're all tasty!*

16-oz. pkg. ground pork
   breakfast sausage
10-3/4 oz. can Cheddar
   cheese soup

2/3 c. water
3 c. biscuit baking mix
1 c. shredded Cheddar cheese

Brown and crumble sausage in a skillet over medium heat; drain and
set aside. In a large bowl, whisk together soup and water until smooth.
Gradually add biscuit mix; stir until well blended. Add sausage and
cheese; stir well until a stiff batter forms. Grease 24 muffin cups. Fill
greased muffin cups 2/3 full. Bake at 350 degrees for 20 to
25 minutes, until golden. Makes 2 dozen.

Breakfast Taters & Bacon

Kathy Milligan
Mira Loma, CA

*I was looking for a good way to use leftover baked potatoes when
I found this marvelous little recipe. Quick & easy.*

4 slices bacon, chopped
1/2 c. onion, chopped
4 baked potatoes, peeled
   and diced

salt and pepper to taste

In a large skillet, cook bacon over medium heat until crisp; partially
drain. Add onion; cook until lightly golden. Add potatoes; season with
salt and pepper. Mix with a spatula to blend. Cook until golden, about
5 minutes. Cut into sections and flip. Keep cooking until heated
through with lots of brown spots, about 8 minutes. Add more salt
and pepper as needed. Makes 4 servings.

Ella's Easy Granola

Lynnette Jones
East Flat Rock, NC

Our son Kyle deserves the credit for this because it is his recipe that he shared with me. It's named for his little girl, who is our granddaughter. This granola is so simple to make ahead and keep on hand. It's very versatile...cut it into granola bars or crumble to use as a yogurt topping. Add any dried fruit you might like too.

4 c. old-fashioned oats,
   uncooked
2/3 c. oil
3 T. water
2/3 c. brown sugar, packed
2 T. molasses

2 T. maple syrup
2 T. chopped pecans
2 T. sliced almonds
1/2 t. cinnamon
1/4 t. salt

Place oats in a large bowl and add oil; mix thoroughly. In a small bowl, mix water with brown sugar. Add to oat mixture along with remaining ingredients; stir thoroughly. Line a 15"x10" jelly-roll pan with aluminum foil for easy clean-up; spray with non-stick vegetable spray. Spread mixture evenly in pan. Bake at 350 degrees for 30 to 35 minutes. Let cool completely; cut into bars or break up into serving-size pieces. Makes 8 to 10 servings.

Are breakfast smoothies a favorite at your house?
Mix them up the night before, then pour into canning jars
and tuck in the fridge. Perfect portions, ready to go!

Breakfast
ON THE GO

Apple Pie Smoothie

Julie Dossantos
Fort Pierce, FL

This is the perfect breakfast smoothie for autumn.
Fruit and protein...a fine way to begin each day!

1 ripe banana, peeled
1/2 Granny Smith apple, peeled,
   cored and coarsely chopped
4-oz. container vanilla yogurt

1/4 c. applesauce
1 t. creamy peanut butter
cinnamon to taste
3 ice cubes

Place all ingredients in a blender and process well. Immediately pour into a chilled tall glass and serve. Makes one serving.

Growing up in the Houston area, there wasn't much of the traditional autumn weather, but we lived on an acre of land full of pine trees and the trees would shed their pointy needles. When the yard started to get covered in brown needles, it was the children's job to rake them up. Since we were not really amused by this, my sister and brother decided to make it more fun by making huge piles of needles and jumping in them! It made the huge chore so much fun! We did this for many years. I can't wait for my children to be old enough to enjoy the feeling of jumping into big piles of pine needles.

–Kathy Carmona, Webster, TX

Cheesy Potato & Ham Scramble

Sue Klapper
Muskego, WI

Ever since a co-worker gave me this recipe, I've been
making it for weekend breakfasts for my family.

8 eggs, beaten
1/4 c. milk
1/4 t. garlic salt
1/4 t. pepper
1/4 c. green onions, thinly sliced

1 T. butter, sliced
1 c. frozen shredded
  hashbrowns
1/2 c. cooked ham, diced
1/3 c. shredded Cheddar cheese

In a bowl, combine eggs, milk and seasonings. Whisk until well
blended. Stir in green onions; set aside. In a large non-stick skillet,
melt butter over medium heat. Add hashbrowns and ham to skillet.
Cook for 6 to 8 minutes, stirring occasionally, until lightly golden. Add
egg mixture to skillet. Cook over medium heat without stirring until
mixture begins to set around the edges and on the bottom. Using a
large spatula, lift and fold the partially cooked egg mixture so
uncooked portion flows underneath. Continue cooking and folding
for 2 to 3 minutes, until eggs are set but still glossy and moist.
Immediately remove from heat; sprinkle with cheese. Serves 4.

Hard-boiled eggs are terrific to have on hand for speedy
breakfasts, easy sandwiches or even a quick nutritious snack.
Use eggs that have been refrigerated at least seven to
ten days...the shells will slip right off.

❧ *Breakfast* ❧
ON THE GO

Easy Egg Bake

Jennie Gist
Gooseberry Patch

*I've made this dish often to share with friends. It just takes
a few minutes to put together and pop in the oven! Change up
the ingredients as you like...sometimes I'll omit the bacon.*

20-oz. pkg. refrigerated diced
    potatoes with onions
6-oz. pkg. precooked bacon
6 to 8 eggs, beaten

1/4 c. milk
salt and pepper to taste
8-oz. pkg. shredded sharp
    Cheddar cheese

Spray a 13"x9" baking pan with non-stick vegetable spray. Spread
potatoes in pan. Using kitchen scissors, snip bacon into pieces over
potatoes. Bake, uncovered, at 350 degrees for about 15 minutes;
remove from oven. Whisk together eggs and milk; pour over baked
layer. Sprinkle with salt, pepper and cheese. Return to oven,
uncovered, for 25 to 30 minutes, until eggs are set and cheese is
melted. Cut into squares. Serves 8.

Brown Sugar Muffins

Jill Ball
Highland, UT

*I like to make a double or triple batch of these muffins to freeze. They
can be popped in the microwave for a minute to reheat. Enjoy a
warm muffin on the way out the door!*

2 c. all-purpose flour
1 c. brown sugar, packed
1 t. baking soda
1/4 t. salt
1/2 c. butter, softened

1 egg, beaten
1 c. milk
1 t. vanilla extract
Optional: 1/2 c. chopped nuts

Combine all ingredients in a large bowl; stir until moistened. Fill
greased muffin cups about 2/3 full. Bake at 375 degrees for 10 to
12 minutes. Makes 2 dozen.

English Cream Scones

Janis Parr
Campbellford, Ontario

These scones are perfect to serve with afternoon tea. They are light and dainty...so good with a dab of homemade strawberry jam.

2 c. all-purpose flour
2 T. sugar
1 T. baking powder
1/2 t. salt
1/4 c. butter

2 eggs
1/3 c. light cream
Garnish: beaten egg white,
    additional sugar

Combine flour, sugar, baking powder and salt. Cut in butter with 2 knives until mixture resembles coarse cornmeal. In a separate bowl, beat eggs until light; stir in cream. Make a well in the center of flour mixture; slowly add egg mixture. Stir vigorously until dough comes away from the side of the bowl. Pat out dough 3/4-inch thick; cut into squares or triangles. Place on a greased baking sheet. Brush tops with beaten egg white; sprinkle with sugar. Bake at 450 degrees for 12 to 15 minutes. Serve warm. Makes 9 to 12.

Maple-Walnutty Spread

Sharon Demers
Dolores, CO

Perfect to spread on piping hot scones in the fall.

8-oz. pkg. cream cheese,
    softened
2 T. maple syrup

1/2 t. maple extract
1/2 c. chopped walnuts, toasted

Beat cream cheese with syrup and extract until well mixed. Fold in walnuts. Let stand 20 to 30 minutes to allow flavors to blend before serving. Keep refrigerated. Makes about 1-1/2 cups.

A basket of homemade scones with a jar of creamy spread makes a tasty teacher gift. Tuck in a tiny slate board as a clever gift tag.

Snacks & Appetizers
TO SHARE

Jack-o'-Lantern Jumble

Carrie Kelderman
Pella, IA

This is a sweet & savory mix that our kids request each fall. Whenever
we share it with our extended family, it's gone in a flash!

8 c. bite-size crispy corn &
   rice cereal squares
1 c. dry-roasted peanuts
1/4 c. butter, sliced

1/4 c. creamy peanut butter
2-1/4 t. Worcestershire sauce
1/4 t. garlic salt
1 to 2 c. candy corn

Combine cereal and peanuts in a large bowl; set aside. In a saucepan, combine remaining ingredients except candy corn. Cook over low heat until melted, stirring frequently. Pour over cereal mixture, stirring to coat well. Spread in a lightly greased 15"x10" jelly-roll pan. Bake, uncovered, at 250 degrees for one hour. Cool to room temperature; stir in candy corn. Store in an airtight container. Makes 10 to 11 cups.

Every fall, our family heads to the local pumpkin patch with the little ones to let them pick a pumpkin. We call it "punkin' huntin'" and the kids love it! When our boys were little, it would be my husband and I taking them to a family farm about an hour from home. Now that they're in high school and college, my sister and I take my youngest granddaughter and anyone else who wants to go. It's a cherished tradition and particularly special to me as fall is my favorite time of year.

–Brenda Lenz, Georgetown, TX

Snacks & Appetizers
❂ TO SHARE ❂

Sticky Popcorn

Brittney Green
Frederick, CO

This is the first snack to go at any get-together! It always brings back special memories from when I was young and my friend's mom would make it for us. I even remember asking her for the recipe when I was ten years old, so my mom could make it for me.

5 to 6 family-size pkgs.
   microwave popcorn, popped
1 c. butter, sliced

1-1/3 c. sugar
1/2 c. light corn syrup
1 t. vanilla extract

Pop popcorn and place in a large heat-proof bowl. Discard any unpopped kernels; set aside. In a heavy saucepan over medium heat, combine butter, sugar and corn syrup. Bring to a boil; cook for about 5 minutes, until mixture reaches the soft-ball stage, or 234 to 243 degrees on a candy thermometer. Remove from heat; stir in vanilla and pour over popcorn. Toss to coat well; spread on wax paper and let cool. Makes 25 servings.

Fall Delight

Jo Ann Belovitch
Stratford, CT

A sweet treat for munching that's ready in just a minute!

1 c. candy-coated chocolates
1 c. candy corn

1 c. cashews
1 c. raisins

Toss together all ingredients in a serving bowl; serve. Makes 4 cups.

Paper cupcake liners come in all colors...great for serving single portions of party mix.

Candy Corn Crispy Balls

Amy Jones
Graham, NC

*A different take on popcorn balls...these are fun,
easy and so delicious!*

4 c. crispy rice cereal
2 c. candy corn
1/2 c. creamy peanut butter

1/4 c. butter, sliced
4 c. mini marshmallows
Optional: cellophane, ribbon

Combine cereal and candy corn in a large bowl; set aside. Melt butter
and peanut butter in a large saucepan over low heat. Add
marshmallows; stir until completely melted. Pour over cereal mixture;
stir to coat. With buttered fingers, roll into balls the size of a tennis
ball. If desired, wrap each ball in an 8-inch square of cellophane;
twist ends closed and tie with ribbon. For a simpler way, press warm
mixture into a buttered 13"x9" baking pan and cut into squares.
Makes 16 balls.

Surprise a friend or neighbor with a homemade popcorn ball
in a trick-or-treat bag! It's so simple. Just place the popcorn
ball in an orange paper bag and gather together the top of
the bag; secure with a rubber band. Hide the rubber
band with green florists' tape.

Spicy Vanilla-Glazed Pretzels

Jonni Sue Wilhelm
Hebron, MD

Every Sunday at church I set out bowls of pretzels for people to snack on with their coffee. This slightly sweet pretzel is a bit spicy too! I like to make one bowlful using sugar and one bowlful using sweetener so that people who need sugar-free snacks can enjoy them too. They have been a big hit!

14-oz. pkg. pretzel sticks or
   mini pretzel twists
2 egg whites
2 T. vanilla extract
1/2 c. sugar, or 3/4 c. powdered
   calorie-free sweetener

1 T. cinnamon
1/2 t. cayenne pepper
1/2 t. salt

Pour pretzels into a large heat-proof bowl; set aside. In a small bowl, beat egg whites and vanilla until foamy; pour over pretzels and toss to coat. In a separate medium bowl, combine sugar or sweetener, spices and salt; mix well. Pour mixture over pretzels; toss again to coat evenly. Spread on a greased 15"x10" jelly-roll pan. Bake, uncovered, at 250 degrees for about one hour; let cool. Break apart. Store in airtight container. Makes 15 to 20 servings.

Family night! Serve a simple supper, then spend
the evening assembling jigsaw puzzles or
playing favorite board games together.

Harvest Apple Cheese Ball

Lorrie Coop
Munday, TX

My daughter Brittany started making this cheese ball as a young 4-H'er as part of her fall foods project. It adds a little whimsy to any holiday table.

8-oz. pkg. cream cheese,
   softened
1 c. shredded Cheddar cheese
1/4 t. cinnamon
3/4 c. dried apples, finely
   chopped

1/3 c. chopped nuts
Garnish: 2-inch cinnamon stick,
   bay leaf
assorted crackers

In a large bowl, beat cream cheese, Cheddar cheese and cinnamon until blended. Stir in dried apples. Form mixture into an apple shape; roll in chopped nuts. Insert cinnamon stick and bay leaf on top to resemble an apple's stem and leaf. Cover and refrigerate until firm. Serve with crackers. Makes 10 servings.

Still too warm for a fire? Give your fireplace a welcoming autumn glow...fill it with pots of flame-colored orange and yellow mums.

Toffee Apple Dip

Kim McCallie
Guyton, GA

My friends & family always request this dip. Chill overnight to soften the toffee bits and create luscious ribbons of toffee.

8-oz. pkg. cream cheese,
   softened
1/4 c. butter, softened
3 T. powdered sugar

1/2 c. brown sugar, packed
1 t. vanilla extract
8-oz. pkg. toffee bits, divided
sliced apples, graham crackers

Combine cream cheese and butter in a large bowl. Beat with an electric mixer on low speed until blended. Add sugars and vanilla; mix well. Set aside 1/4 cup toffee bits; add remaining toffee bits to cream cheese mixture. Stir until well blended. Cover and refrigerate overnight, if possible. Just before serving, sprinkle remaining toffee bits on top of dip. Serve with sliced apples and graham crackers for dipping. Serves 8 to 10.

A tried & true kid craft...leaf art! Have kids hunt for colorful leaves, then press the leaves in a heavy book between pieces of wax paper for a few days. Glue leaves to colored paper to form a picture. Twigs, seed pods and acorn caps can be added too. Finish by drawing on details.

Cranberry-Jalapeño Salsa

Bonnie Waters
Bloomington, IN

This salsa has been a family favorite at Thanksgiving and other gatherings for many years. I have to make two or three batches! We grow our own jalapeños and green onions, so when in season, it's fresh from our garden. This salsa is also delicious as a sauce over roast turkey or pork for a meal or sandwich.

14-oz. can whole-berry
   cranberry sauce
1 jalapeño pepper, halved,
   seeded and diced
1/4 c. fresh cilantro, snipped

2 green onions, sliced
1 t. lime juice
1/4 t. ground cumin
tortilla chips

In a bowl, combine all ingredients except tortilla chips. Stir until well blended. Serve at room temperature or cover and chill. Serve with tortilla chips. Makes 8 servings.

Plenty of ready-to-eat goodies can be found at farmers' markets and roadside stands. Tuck a basket filled with picnic supplies into the car trunk along with a quilt to sit on. Instant picnic!

Snacks & Appetizers
☼ TO SHARE ☼

Cheesy Jack-o'-Lantern

Lori Simmons
Princeville, IL

This cheese ball looks just like a pumpkin...great for Halloween!
If you have extra pepperoni, chop it finely and stir into
the cream cheese mixture for a tasty addition.

3 green onions, divided
2 8-oz. pkgs. cream cheese,
  softened
8-oz. pkg. shredded Cheddar
  cheese, divided

1/4 c. red pepper, finely chopped
Garnish: several slices pepperoni
assorted crackers

Cut a 4-inch "stem" from the green part of one onion; chop remaining onions and set aside. In a bowl, beat together cream cheese and 1-1/4 cups Cheddar cheese. Stir in remaining onions and red pepper; cover and refrigerate one hour. Form into a ball; roll in remaining Cheddar cheese. Cut pepperoni slices into triangle shapes for eyes, nose and mouth; press into cheese ball to make a face. Insert reserved onion piece into top. Makes 3 cups.

Pepper Jelly Cream Cheese

Holly Child
Parker, CO

With just a few ingredients on hand, I can always whip up this
quick appetizer for any type of gathering. Easy to put together
and always a big hit with its spicy-sweet flavor.

8-oz. pkg. cream cheese,
  softened
1/4 c. medium salsa

1/4 c. orange marmalade
assorted crackers

Unwrap cream cheese and place the block on a serving dish. Mix together salsa and marmalade in a bowl; spoon evenly over cream cheese. Serve with assorted crackers. Makes 10 to12 servings.

43

Glazed Sausage Balls

*Beth Wajts
Sterling Forest, NY*

This is a terrific appetizer for watching those football games that have you sitting on the edge of your seat, or a fun night at home playing games and sharing snacks with friends.

16-oz. pkg. ground hot
   pork sausage
1 egg, beaten
2 c. saltine crackers, finely
   crushed

2-1/2 c. tomato juice, divided
2 T. oil
3/4 c. brown sugar, packed
1/4 c. vinegar
2 T. dry mustard

In a large bowl, combine sausage, egg, crackers and 1/2 cup tomato juice. Mix well; form into small meatballs. In a large skillet, brown meatballs in oil; drain and set aside. Add remaining tomato juice and other ingredients to skillet; mix well. Return meatballs to tomato mixture. Reduce heat to medium-low. Cover and simmer for about 30 minutes. May be kept warm in a slow cooker on low setting. Makes about 3 dozen.

Pick up a dozen pint-size Mason jars for entertaining...
they're fun and practical for serving frosty root beer
or chilled apple cider.

Barbecue Drummies

Debi King
Reisterstown, MD

My friend Sharon gave me the idea of using drumsticks instead of wings, since they are less messy. I like to pack the baking dish of drummies in a portable carrier to take to football games.

14-oz. can whole-berry
  cranberry sauce
12-oz. bottle chili sauce
2 T. red pepper flakes

3 lbs. chicken drumsticks
2 T. olive oil
Garnish: ranch or blue cheese
  salad dressing, celery sticks

Combine cranberry sauce, chili sauce and red pepper flakes in a one-gallon plastic zipping bag. Knead bag to mix. Remove 1/2 cup of sauce mixture and refrigerate. Pat drumsticks dry with a paper towel; add to bag. Seal bag and refrigerate for at least one hour. Remove drumsticks to a greased 13"x9" glass baking pan, discarding sauce mixture in bag. Bake, uncovered, at 375 degrees for about 25 minutes. Turn drumsticks over; baste with reserved sauce mixture. Bake for another 7 to 10 minutes, until chicken juices run clear. Serve drumsticks with salad dressing and celery sticks for dipping. Makes 8 to 12 servings.

Packing for a picnic or a tailgating party? Safety first!
Keep hot foods hot, cold foods cold, and don't let any food
sit out longer than 2 hours, even if the food looks just fine.

Smoked Pimento Cheese Dip

Mary Bettuchy
Columbia, SC

We're a military family, so we've been stationed all over the country and get to try different regional foods. Here in South Carolina, one of the most delicious things I've discovered is pimento cheese! The smoky flavor is my own spin on this classic.

8-oz. pkg. smoked Cheddar
  cheese, shredded
8-oz. pkg. cream cheese,
  softened
2 4-oz. jars pimentos or
  roasted red peppers, drained
  and diced

1/4 c. mayonnaise
1/2 t. smoked salt or
  1/4 t. smoke-flavored
  cooking sauce
1/4 t. hot pepper sauce
1/4 t. red pepper flakes
pita chips

In a food processor or blender, combine all ingredients except pita chips. Pulse until combined. If mixture is too thick, add a little more mayonnaise. If more smoky flavor or heat is desired, add more smoke or hot sauce to taste. Serve with pita chips. Serves 8.

Tasty Bread Spread

Beckie Apple
Grannis, AR

*Tuck this savory spread in the fridge for those hurry-up days
when you want to enjoy something special.*

2 c. finely shredded mozzarella
  or Parmesan cheese
4-1/4 oz. can chopped black
  olives, drained
1 c. butter, softened

1 c. mayonnaise
1 t. minced garlic or garlic
  powder
split rolls or sliced French bread

Combine all ingredients except rolls or bread and mix well. Cover and chill for one to 2 hours. To serve, spread on split or sliced dinner rolls or French bread. Place on an aluminum foil-lined baking sheet. Bake at 375 degrees for 20 to 25 minutes, until toasted. Cover and refrigerate up to 2 weeks. Makes about 4 cups.

Homemade Boursin Cheese

Denise Webb
Newington, GA

*Boursin cheese is a little pricey for me, so I was thrilled
to find this recipe to make my own. It's wonderful on
crackers and fabulous in sausage cheese balls.*

2 8-oz. pkgs. cream cheese,
   softened
8-oz. container whipped butter,
   room temperature
1 t. garlic salt
1/2 t. dried oregano

1/4 t. dried marjoram
1/4 t. dried thyme
1/4 t. dried basil
1/4 t. dill weed
1/4 t. pepper

Combine all ingredients in a food processor or blender. Process until
completely blended and smooth. Line a serving bowl with plastic
wrap; spoon cheese mixture into bowl. Cover and refrigerate for
several hours before serving, to allow flavors to blend. Makes 3 cups.

Need to soften cream cheese in a hurry? Simply place
an unwrapped 8-ounce block on a plate and microwave
for about a minute at 50% power.

Monterey Mushroom Squares

JoAnn

*These cheesy squares are irresistible! Mix & match
different kinds of mushrooms and cheeses for variety.*

8-oz. tube refrigerated
  crescent rolls
2 c. sliced mushrooms
1/4 c. butter, melted

1/2 c. shredded Monterey Jack
  cheese
1/2 t. dried oregano
1/4 t. onion salt

Separate rolls into 2 long rectangles. Press into the bottom and 1/2-
inch up the sides of a lightly greased 13"x9" baking pan. Toss
mushrooms with melted butter; spoon over dough. Sprinkle with
remaining ingredients. Bake, uncovered, at 375 degrees for 20 to
25 minutes. Cut into squares; serve warm. Makes 2 dozen.

Savory Spinach Rolls

*Laurie Rupsis
Aiken, SC*

*I bring these to our church's potlucks but never set them out before
the crowd comes in. The ladies working the kitchen seem to
eat a lot of them before the potluck even starts!*

2 onions, chopped
3/4 c. butter
2 10-oz. pkgs frozen spinach
3 c. stuffing mix

6 eggs, beaten
1/2 c. shredded Parmesan
  cheese

In a skillet over medium heat, sauté onions in butter until tender.
Cook spinach according to package directions; squeeze dry. In a bowl,
combine onion mixture, spinach and remaining ingredients. Shape
into 2-inch balls using a cookie scoop. Refrigerate at least one hour,
until firm. Place on a lightly greased baking sheet. Bake, uncovered,
at 350 degrees for 20 minutes. May be frozen unbaked; bake just
before serving. Serve warm or cool. Makes 3 dozen.

Country Caviar

Kay Pyle
Stockton, MO

One of our favorite dips! It's easy to make and keeps for days in the fridge, if it lasts that long. I have made it for ages and my grandkids love it. Great for family gatherings and football games. Spice it to suit to your taste, from mild to extra hot.

15-oz. can black, red or
    pinto beans, drained
11-oz. can sweet corn & diced
    peppers, drained
10-oz. can mild, medium or
    hot diced tomatoes with
    green chiles, drained
6 green onions, chopped

2 c. shredded Monterey Jack,
    Pepper Jack or Cheddar
    cheese
1 c. light mayonnaise
1 c. light sour cream
hot pepper sauce to taste
pita chips, tortilla chips

Mix together all ingredients except chips in a large bowl. Cover and chill; may be kept refrigerated for several days. Serve with warm pita chips or tortilla chips. Serves 8 to 10.

Make your own crunchy pita chips for dipping. Cut pita bread rounds into triangles, brush lightly with olive oil and sprinkle with garlic salt or herbs. Bake at 350 degrees for a few minutes, until crisp.

Corn Dog Muffins

Tina Goodpasture
Meadowview, VA

I love hot dogs any way that I can find to fix them.
This recipe is fast, easy and good!

6 hot dogs
1 c. all-purpose flour
1 c. cornmeal
1/2 c. sugar
2-1/2 t. baking powder
1 t. salt

1 c. milk
1/3 c. oil
1 egg
Garnish: catsup, mustard,
    pickle relish

In a skillet over medium heat, cook hot dogs for 5 to 8 minutes, just until starting to brown. Remove from heat. Cut each hot dog into 6 pieces; set aside. In a large bowl, combine flour, cornmeal, sugar, baking powder and salt. Add egg, milk and oil; stir until just combined. Spray mini muffin cups with non-stick vegetable spray. Spoon batter into muffin cups, filling 2/3 full. Press one piece of hot dog into the center of each muffin cup. Bake at 350 degrees for 10 minutes. Increase heat to 400 degrees. Bake another 3 to 5 minutes, watching closely, until golden. Cool in muffin tins for 5 minutes before removing. Serve muffins with your favorite condiments. Makes 3 dozen.

A muffin tin makes a terrific condiment server. Fill each cup with something different...how about catsup, mustard, relish, hot pepper sauce, horseradish and mayonnaise?

Meatball Sliders

Becky Drees
Pittsfield, MA

So easy to make...a big hit at football parties!

32 frozen Italian-style meatballs
28-oz. jar pasta sauce
2 8-oz. tubes refrigerated
   crescent rolls

11 slices mozzarella cheese,
   cut into thirds

Combine meatballs and sauce in a large saucepan. Simmer over low heat until warmed through, 5 to 10 minutes. Separate crescent rolls into triangles. Cut each triangle in half width-wise to form 2 triangles. Top each triangle with 1/3 slice cheese and one meatball; roll up. Bake, uncovered, at 375 degrees for 15 to 18 minutes, until golden. Makes 32 sliders.

When I was growing up, I couldn't wait until I was old enough to join the Grange. In the fall when the weather was crisp and trees were so beautiful, the Grange members would have a picnic. Some of the younger members would go ahead to the park and get the fire going for the delicious hot dogs and hamburgers. Then the ladies came, bringing all those luscious covered dishes for a wonderful feast. While they got the meal ready, the men would pitch horseshoes. The kids played hide & seek and put on skits. Then we all ate until we were stuffed! These are some of my best memories.

–Barbara Feldner, Caldwell, OH

Bacon-Wrapped Pineapple Bites

Jessica Kraus
Delaware, OH

These are so irresistible...the mixture of salty and sweet is amazing!
You should probably double the recipe, because they'll go quickly.

1 c. brown sugar, packed
16-oz. pkg. bacon, slices cut
   in half
20-oz. can pineapple chunks,
   drained

wooden toothpicks, soaked
   in water

Place brown sugar in a shallow bowl. Dredge each half-slice of bacon
in brown sugar. Place one pineapple chunk on one end of each
bacon piece and roll up; secure with a toothpick. Sprinkle rolls with
remaining brown sugar. Arrange on a greased rack placed on a baking
sheet. Bake at 375 degrees for 25 minutes, or until bacon is crisp.
Makes 10 servings.

Smoked Kielbasa Bites

Marcia Shaffer
Conneaut Lake, PA

Perfect for football snacking!

1 lb. Kielbasa sausage, cut into
   bite-size pieces
3/4 c. ginger ale

1/2 c. brown sugar, packed
1/2 c. barbecue sauce

Place sausage in a greased 9"x9" baking pan. Mix together ginger ale,
brown sugar and barbecue sauce; spoon over sausage. Cover; bake at
300 degrees for 1-1/2 hours. Serves 6.

For a fun after-school snack
that's ready in a jiffy, stuff a
hollowed-out apple with
peanut butter and raisins.

Snacks & Appetizers
☉ TO SHARE ☉

Ranch Buffalo Wings

Phyl Broich-Wessling
Garner, IA

We love chicken wing appetizers for parties and snacks, so I'm always on the lookout for a new recipe to try, the easier the better. This one is very tasty...the secret ingredient is the vinegar.

1/2 c. butter, melted
1/4 c. hot pepper sauce,
   or to taste
3 T. white vinegar
12 chicken wings,
   cut into sections

1-oz. pkg. ranch salad
   dressing mix
1/2 t. paprika
Garnish: ranch salad dressing,
   celery sticks

In a small bowl, whisk together butter, hot sauce and vinegar. Dip wing pieces into butter mixture. Arrange in a single layer on a large cast-iron pizza pan or other baking pan. Sprinkle with salad dressing mix. Bake, uncovered, at 350 degrees for 30 to 40 minutes, until wings are golden and juices run clear, basting occasionally with pan juices. Sprinkle with paprika. Serve wings with salad dressing and celery sticks for dipping. Serves 6 to 8.

Wondering what's the best way to cut up slippery chicken wings? A pair of sturdy kitchen scissors does the job in a jiffy. Afterwards, wash the scissors well in soapy water and set on a towel to dry.

53

Texas Snacker Crackers

Kim Hinshaw
Cedar Park, TX

*When I served these to my bunco group, everyone wanted to play
at the table with the spicy crackers! Store-brand crackers
work great, so save yourself a little cash.*

2 c. canola oil
1-oz. pkg. ranch salad
   dressing mix
3 T. red pepper flakes

2 T. paprika
2 t. garlic, minced
16-oz. pkg. saltine crackers,
   divided

Whisk together oil, dressing mix and seasonings in a bowl, adjusting
spices to suit your taste. Add one sleeve of crackers to a one-gallon
plastic zipping bag; pour 1/4 of oil mixture over crackers. Alternately
repeat with remaining 3 sleeves and oil mixture. Seal bag. Let stand
for 24 hours, turning bag over once every hour. Makes 30 servings of
5 crackers each.

Slow-Cooked Chili Peanuts

Paula Marchesi
Huntsville, PA

*I love fixing quick & easy appetizers, especially during football
season. These nuts are simply awesome! You'll love the taste
and how easy they are to prepare.*

2 12-oz. cans cocktail peanuts
1/4 c. butter, melted

1-5/8 oz. pkg. chili seasoning
mix

Place peanuts in a slow cooker. Drizzle with melted butter; sprinkle
with seasoning mix. Toss together. Cover and cook on low setting for
2 to 2-1/2 hours. Uncover and turn to high setting; cook another
10 to 15 minutes. Serve warm or cool. Makes about 5 cups.

*For stand-up parties, make it easy on guests by serving foods
that can be eaten in just one or two bites.*

Candied Nuts

JoAnne Hayon
Sheboygan, WI

My husband and I attended a Toys for Tots party and these nuts were going like wildfire. I knew I needed to get the recipe! Very tasty for fall and winter holidays...makes a nice hostess gift.

3 c. peanuts, mixed nuts
  or almonds
1 egg
1 t. salt
1 c. powdered calorie-free
  sweetener

Optional: 1 to 2 t. pumpkin
  pie spice or cinnamon
6 T. butter, sliced

Spread nuts on an ungreased baking sheet. Bake, uncovered, at 300 degrees for 15 minutes, or until warmed. Meanwhile, in a large bowl, beat egg and salt until foamy. Add sweetener and spice, if desired. Add warmed nuts to egg mixture; stir to coat. Melt butter in a disposable 13"x9" aluminum baking pan in the oven; spread nuts in pan. Bake, uncovered, at 300 degrees for 30 minutes, stirring every 6 to 7 minutes. Drain nuts on paper towels. Store in an airtight container. Makes about 3 cups.

For a quick & easy snack that everybody loves, nothing beats a big bowl of popcorn. Jazz it up with a sprinkle of grated Parmesan cheese or taco seasoning mix, or serve it the classic way, with butter and salt.

Kevin's Football Dip

Diana Karol
Dickerson, KS

Sunday afternoon football games wouldn't be the same without this hearty dip. Kevin is our son-in-law and the go-to guy for crowd-pleasers. A slow cooker makes this dip so easy!

1 lb. ground beef
1/2 c. onion, chopped
8-oz. jar taco sauce
10-oz. can diced tomatoes with
   hot peppers

32-oz. pkg. pasteurized process
   cheese spread, cubed
tortilla chips, cubed French
   bread

Brown beef with onion in a skillet over medium heat; drain. Transfer beef mixture to a slow cooker; add taco sauce, tomatoes and cheese. Cover and cook on high setting for about 45 minutes, stirring every 10 minutes, until cheese is completely melted. Reduce heat to low setting; serve with chips and bread cubes. Makes 10 to 12 servings.

If busy kids can't get home for dinner, take it to them.
Pack a tailgating basket and enjoy picnicking with them at
the stadium. Be sure to pack extra for hungry team members!

Snacks & Appetizers
✿ TO SHARE ✿

Border Bites

Amy Hunt
Traphill, NC

*My family loves Mexican dip! These zesty bites are
just the right size for snacking.*

24 wonton wrappers	1 c. shredded Mexican-blend
1 c. canned refried beans	cheese
1/4 to 1/2 c. salsa	Garnish: sour cream, diced
1 T. taco seasoning mix	tomato, diced green onions

Spray 24 mini muffin cups with non-stick vegetable spray. Gently
press a wonton wrapper into each cup, with edges extending over
top of cups. Bake at 350 degrees for 5 minutes; let cool. Combine
beans, salsa and seasoning mix; spoon mixture into cups. Bake at
350 degrees for 10 minutes, or until heated through. Top with cheese
and bake one to 2 minutes more, until cheese melts. Garnish as
desired. Makes 2 dozen.

Cheesy Chile Artichoke Dip

Hollie Moots
Marysville, OH

*This has become a staple at our get-togethers. It's so easy
to prepare...and once you've tried it, you can't stop dipping!*

14-oz. jar artichokes, drained	4-oz. can green chiles
and chopped	1/4 c. mayonnaise
6-1/2 oz. jar marinated	2 c. shredded Cheddar cheese
artichokes, drained	tortilla chips, snack crackers
and chopped	

Combine artichokes, chiles, mayonnaise and cheese in a bowl; mix
well. Transfer to a greased 8"x8" baking pan. Bake, uncovered, at
350 degrees for 20 to 25 minutes, until bubbly and cheese is melted.
Serve with tortilla chips and crackers. Serves 10 to 12.

Sarah's Special Pickles

Sarah Slaven
Strunk, KY

These fried pickles are great year 'round, but especially for tailgating, homecoming and other fall activities. Try them with homemade ranch dip on the side...yum!

1 c. cornmeal
1 c. self-rising flour
1 t. garlic powder
1 t. onion powder
1/2 t. salt

1 t. pepper
3 eggs
32-oz. jar hamburger dill pickle
    chips, well drained
oil for frying

Combine cornmeal, flour and seasonings in a shallow bowl; beat eggs in a separate shallow bowl. Coat pickle chips in cornmeal mixture, then dip in eggs. Coat again in cornmeal mixture and eggs; coat once more in cornmeal mixture. In a stockpot, heat 2 inches oil to about 375 degrees. Working in batches, add pickles to oil. Cook for about 2 minutes, until golden on both sides. Drain on paper towels. Makes 12 servings.

ooompah!

On a sunny autumn day, throw a backyard Oktoberfest party! Set a festive mood with polka music. Toss some brats on the grill to serve in hard rolls, topped with sauerkraut. Round out the menu with potato salad, homemade applesauce and German chocolate cake for dessert. Sure to be fun for all!

Sweet & Spicy Pickles

*Shirley Morris
Clarks Summit, PA*

*I first tried this recipe for a Fathers' Day gift and
25 years later, it's still my most-requested recipe.*

32-oz. jar whole dill pickles,
   drained, rinsed and sliced
3 to 4 heatproof plastic or
   glass containers with lids
1/2 c. red wine vinegar

2 c. sugar
1 t. celery seed
1 t. dry mustard
3/4 t. red pepper flakes
1/8 t. garlic salt

Pack pickle slices into containers; set aside. Combine remaining
ingredients in a saucepan over medium-high heat; bring to a boil.
Remove from heat; let cool. Ladle equal amounts of vinegar mixture
into each container; let cool. Add lids. Refrigerate for 2 weeks before
serving, if possible, to allow flavors to blend. May be kept refrigerated
for 8 weeks. Makes about 12 servings.

The leaves had a wonderful frolic,
They danced to the wind's loud song.
They whirled, and they floated and scampered,
They circled and flew along.

– Anonymous

Crabmeat Party Spread

Pearl Teiserskas
Brookfield, IL

I received this recipe from a friend back in 1975. Originally I took it to holiday parties, now my family & friends make this for any occasion when they all get together. There are never any leftovers.

1-1/2 c. cream cheese, softened
2 T. mayonnaise-style salad
   dressing
1/2 c. onion, minced
1 clove garlic, minced

juice of 1/2 lemon
3/4 c. chili sauce
1 lb. imitation crabmeat, diced
crackers or celery sticks

In a bowl, combine cream cheese, salad dressing, onion, garlic and lemon juice. Blend well and spread on a serving platter. Top with chili sauce; sprinkle with crabmeat. Serve with crackers or celery sticks. Makes 10 servings.

Blanching makes fresh veggies crisp and bright...super for dipping. Bring a large pot of salted water to a rolling boil, add trimmed veggies and boil for 3 to 4 minutes, just until they begin to soften. Immediately remove veggies to a bowl of ice water. Cool, drain and pat dry.

Hot Shrimp & Artichoke Dip

Char Frojen
Missoula, MT

Sure to be a hit at your next get-together!

16-oz. container sour cream
1 c. mayonnaise
8-oz. pkg. cream cheese,
  softened
2 6-oz. cans medium shrimp,
  drained

4-oz. can sliced black olives,
  drained
4-oz. jar marinated artichokes,
  drained and shredded
assorted crackers

In a bowl, blend together sour cream, mayonnaise and cream cheese. Stir in shrimp, olives and artichokes; transfer to a lightly greased 8"x8" glass baking pan. Bake, uncovered, at 350 degrees for 30 minutes. Serve warm with crackers. Makes about 4 cups.

Shrimp Dip à la Lory

Lory Howard
Jackson, CA

A great tailgate recipe...so easy, so good!

6-oz. can medium shrimp,
  drained
1 c. mayonnaise
1 c. shredded Cheddar cheese

1 T. onion, grated
1/8 t. Worcestershire sauce
1/8 t. salt
assorted crackers

Blend all ingredients except crackers in a bowl. Cover and chill until serving time. Serve with crackers. Makes 6 to 8 servings.

A good rule of thumb for appetizers...allow 6 to 8 servings per person if dinner will follow. Plan for 12 to 15 per person if it's an appetizer-only gathering.

Not Just Any Cheese Ball

JoAnn Kurtz
Castaic, CA

This recipe was given to me by a co-worker 15 years ago. I've used it for parties of all kinds and even given it as a hostess gift.

2 8-oz. pkgs. cream cheese, softened
1-1/2 T. ranch salad dressing mix
1/2 c. celery, finely chopped

3 T. dried, minced onion
1/2 t. granulated garlic, or more to taste
1 c. salted peanuts, chopped
snack crackers

In a bowl, mix all ingredients except peanuts and crackers; form into a ball. Wrap in plastic wrap and refrigerate. At serving time, roll cheese ball in chopped peanuts. Serve with crackers. Makes 12 servings.

Spoon dips and spreads into pretty crocks or vintage blue canning jars...they're ideal as hostess gifts. Add a box of crisp crackers and tie on a spreader with a pretty ribbon... sure to be appreciated!

Snacks & Appetizers
☺ TO SHARE ☺

Mediterranean Stuffed Mushrooms

Joyceann Dreibelbis
Wooster, OH

These delicious mushrooms can be stuffed in advance. Prep time is only 30 minutes! For best results, use mushrooms with caps that are about two inches in diameter.

16 mushrooms, stems removed
1 T. olive oil
1/4 c. sun-dried tomatoes in oil,
  drained and finely chopped
1/2 c. panko dry bread crumbs

1 green onion, thinly sliced
1/2 c. cream cheese, softened
1/2 c. shredded 3-cheese blend
1 T. fresh basil, chopped

Finely chop enough mushroom stems to measure 1/4 cup. Discard any remaining stems. Heat oil in a skillet over medium-high heat. Add chopped stems and tomatoes; cook and stir for 2 to 4 minutes. Add bread crumbs and onion; cook and stir for one minute. Remove from heat; let cool for 10 minutes. Set aside 1/4 cup crumb mixture for topping. In a bowl, mix cream cheese, shredded cheese and basil until blended. Stir in remaining crumb mixture; spoon into mushroom caps, adding about one tablespoon of mixture to each. Arrange mushroom caps on an aluminum foil-lined rimmed baking sheet; sprinkle with reserved crumb mixture. Bake at 400 degrees for 15 to 20 minutes, until heated through. Makes 16 mushrooms.

Make a party tray of savory bite-size appetizer tarts...guests will never suspect how easy it is! Bake frozen mini phyllo shells according to package directions, then spoon in a favorite creamy dip or spread.

63

Marcie's Autumn Tea

Leona Krivda
Belle Vernon, PA

*My oldest daughter makes this refreshing chilled tea in the fall
and it is always a hit. We hope you will enjoy it also.*

5 tea bags
1/2 c. sugar
5 c. boiling water
5 c. unsweetened apple juice

2 c. cranberry juice cocktail
1/3 c. lemon juice
1/4 t. pumpkin pie spice
ice cubes

Combine tea bags and sugar in a heat-proof one-gallon pitcher. Add
boiling water; let stand for 8 minutes. Discard tea bags. Add juices
and spice; stir well until sugar is dissolved. Chill; serve over ice.
Makes about 3 quarts.

Big, colorful ice cubes for a party punch bowl...
arrange fresh cranberries or thin slices of citrus in
muffin tins, fill with water and freeze.

Harvest Moon Punch

Sandy Ward
Anderson, IN

*This refreshing punch is super-simple to stir up
and will serve a thirsty crowd.*

2 qts. apple cider
1 c. lemon juice

1/2 c. sugar
2 ltrs. ginger ale, chilled

In a punch bowl or large pitcher, combine cider, lemon juice and sugar. Stir until sugar dissolves. Cover and chill. Add ginger ale just before serving. Makes about one gallon.

When I was young, my parents and I would go to my aunt's & uncle's house for Thanksgiving dinner. An elderly neighbor couple and a bachelor neighbor were also invited to share the day. Usually there were 12 to 16 people sitting down to the table. My aunt is a fantastic cook and this was her day to indulge her love of cooking. Besides two roast turkeys, two kinds of stuffing, homemade pickles, pickled beets, applesauce and cranberry relish, there were usually a dozen different pies, cakes, tartlets and cheesecake. Needless to say, we would return for the next two days to finish up all the delicious food. These days, Thanksgiving is a much smaller affair. Even though now it's just my parents, my fiancé and me, I have fond memories of those large dinners with all that wonderful food.

–Lisa Cunningham, Boothbay, ME

Hot Caramel Apple Cider

Jessica Shrout
Flintstone, MD

This slow-cooker beverage is great on cool fall days. A sweet pick-me-up that everyone will love...it's so easy to whip up and go about your day!

3 qts. apple cider or apple juice
6 4-inch cinnamon sticks
1/2 c. caramel ice cream topping

Garnish: whipped cream, additional caramel topping

Pour apple juice or cider into a slow cooker; add cinnamon sticks. Cover and cook on high setting for about 4 hours. Cinnamon sticks will soften and uncurl. Just before serving, stir in 1/2 cup caramel topping. Serve in mugs, topped with a dollop of whipped cream and a drizzle of caramel topping. Serves 12.

Autumn is the perfect time of year to hit all the best craft shows, flea markets and tag sales. Call your best girlfriends, pack a basket of snacks and a thermos of spiced cider, and head out for a day of shopping fun.

QUICK
Sandwiches &
Soups

Buffalo Chicken Cheesesteak Sandwiches

Becky Drees
Pittsfield, MA

A favorite football game meal at our house.

1 T. butter, sliced
1 sweet onion, thinly sliced
1 lb. boneless, skinless chicken
   breasts, thinly sliced
salt and pepper to taste

1/2 c. favorite buffalo wing
   sauce
8 slices provolone cheese
4 sub sandwich rolls, split

Melt butter in a large skillet over medium-high heat. Add onion; sauté until golden, about 3 minutes. Season chicken slices with salt and pepper; add to skillet and sauté until no longer pink. Stir in sauce. With a spatula, separate chicken mixture in skillet into 4 portions; top each with 2 cheese slices. Remove skillet from heat; cover and let stand until cheese melts, about 5 minutes. Scoop each cheese-topped section onto a roll; wrap rolls tightly in aluminum foil. Place rolls on a baking sheet. Bake at 250 degrees for 10 minutes, or until warmed through. Unwrap carefully and serve. Makes 4 servings.

Slip children's drawings between two pieces of clear self-adhesive plastic for placemats that are both practical and playful.

⚬ QUICK ⚬
Sandwiches & Soups

Easy Meatball Hoagies

Donna Wilson
Maryville, TN

*Really quick & easy! I love meatball subs and this is
a great recipe to make at home.*

12-oz. pkg. frozen meatballs
24-oz. jar spaghetti sauce
2 T. butter, softened
1/2 t. garlic powder

4 hoagie rolls, split
1/2 c. shredded mozzarella
   cheese

In a saucepan over medium-low heat, combine meatballs and sauce.
Cover and cook for about 15 minutes, stirring occasionally, until
meatballs are cooked. Meanwhile, blend butter and garlic powder in a
small bowl. Partially open rolls; spread cut sides with butter mixture.
Place rolls on a baking sheet. Bake, uncovered, at 350 degrees for
10 minutes, or until toasted. To serve, divide meatballs and sauce
among rolls; sprinkle with cheese. Bake 8 to 10 minutes. Serves 4.

Take the kids to a neighborhood garden center for fall fun...
all-you-can-carry pumpkins, shiny gourds, corn shocks for the
porch posts and maybe even a cup of cool cider. While you're
there, pick out some daffodil bulbs to plant in October.

Mom's Pizza Subs

Debra Stephens
Owasso, OK

This recipe was created by my mother. When I was little, we had one small pizza joint in town. We loved their pizza subs, but they didn't stay in business long. When they closed, Mom studied the ingredients and we made our own at home.

16-oz. pkg. ground pork
   sausage
6-oz. can tomato paste
1/4 c. water
1 t. garlic powder

1 t. dried oregano
8 hamburger buns, split
8 slices provolone cheese
40 pepperoni slices

Brown sausage in a skillet over medium heat; drain. Stir in tomato paste, water and seasonings. Simmer for 5 minutes, or until thickened. Spoon sausage mixture onto bottoms of buns; top each with 5 pepperoni slices and one cheese slice. Add tops of buns; wrap each bun in aluminum foil. Place buns on a baking sheet. Bake at 350 degrees for 10 minutes, or until cheese melts. Unwrap carefully and serve. Makes 8 servings.

Try something new for brown-bag lunches...roll any combination of cheese, deli meat and veggies in a tortilla. Even a kid-friendly peanut butter & jelly wrap tastes terrific!

Mothers' Club Bar-B-Q

Sandy J. Ward
Brimfield, IL

When I was growing up in a small town in the 60s, our school had no cafeteria. It was a real treat when our Mothers' Club sold these sandwiches once a month as a fundraiser. For our family, my mother tweaked it into a recipe using just one pound of hamburger. Now my own daughter requests this every year for her birthday.

1 lb. ground beef
1 onion, chopped
1/2 c. barbecue sauce
1/3 c. brown sugar, packed
1/4 c. catsup

1 T. mustard
1 t. garlic, minced
1 t. vinegar
salt and pepper to taste
4 to 6 hamburger buns, split

Brown beef and onion in a skillet over medium heat; drain. Stir in remaining ingredients except buns; reduce heat to medium-low. Simmer for about 30 minutes, stirring occasionally. If making several batches, mixture may be kept in a slow cooker on low setting for up to 2 hours. Serve on buns. Makes 4 to 6 servings.

Autumn means shopping for new back-to-school clothing. Preserve the memories in children's outgrown clothing by making a simple lap quilt. Cut large squares and stitch together, then layer with thin batting and a fabric backing. So sweet!

Halloween Sloppy Joes

Jessica Kraus
Delaware, OH

A staple at my house for Halloween night. This recipe is so simple and I always have everything I need on hand. I never use canned Sloppy Joe sauce anymore!

1 lb. ground beef	2 T. brown sugar, packed
1 onion, chopped	1 T. cider vinegar
1 c. catsup	1 t. Worcestershire sauce
1/4 c. water	6 hamburger buns, split

Brown beef and onion in a skillet over medium heat; drain. Stir in remaining ingredients except buns; reduce heat to medium-low. Simmer for 25 minutes, stirring occasionally. To serve, spoon onto buns. Makes 6 servings.

When I was a child, my grandmother and mother always made my costumes for Halloween. So when I became a mother, I knew I wanted my children to have homemade costumes too. Of course, I did not take into account the fact that my grandmother was a master seamstress and I could barely sew on a button! Nevertheless, I did my best and made my boys everything from clowns to scarecrows to Frosty the Snowman. My youngest son even won our local costume parade contest when he was just a year old! They're too old to dress up for Halloween anymore, but the memories of making those costumes, then seeing them so excited to put them on, will be with me forever. I hope that my kids keep those memories too, and maybe will carry on the tradition of Halloween costumes, not from a box, but from the heart.

–Hollie Moots, Marysville, OH

○ QUICK ○
Sandwiches & Soups

Cheese Frenchies

Brenda Schlosser
Brighton, CO

Back in the 60s and 70s, a restaurant chain called King's Food Host served these delicious crunchy-gooey sandwiches. The restaurants are no longer around, but these are just as good, if not better! Perfect comfort food on a cold day with a hot bowl of tomato soup.

6 slices white bread	3/4 c. all-purpose flour
3 T. mayonnaise	1 t. salt
6 slices American cheese	1 c. corn flake cereal, crushed
1 egg	oil for deep frying
1/2 c. milk	

Spread bread slices with mayonnaise on one side. Add 2 slices cheese to each of 3 slices; close sandwiches with remaining bread. Cut sandwiches into triangles; trim off crusts, if desired. Whisk together egg, milk, flour and salt in a shallow dish; place crushed cereal in a separate dish. Dip each triangle into egg mixture; coat with cereal. Add one inch oil to a skillet over medium-high heat; heat to 375 degrees. Add triangles; deep-fry until golden on both sides. Place on paper towels to drain. Serves 3.

How do you know when the oil is hot enough for deep-frying? Drop a cube of bread into the hot oil. If it sizzles and turns golden in 60 seconds, the oil is ready to go.

State Fair Italian Sausages

Tamela James
Grove City, OH

This recipe is inspired by our family's many trips to the Ohio State Fair. We love the Italian sausages sold at the fair, but we don't care for the grilled onions and peppers, so we improvised with our own toppings. The contrast of the hot spicy sausages with the cold crisp lettuce is delicious.

6 to 8 Italian pork sausage links   6 to 8 hot dog buns, split
1/2 head lettuce, shredded   mustard to taste
zesty Italian salad dressing
   to taste

In a large saucepan, cover sausages with water. Bring to a boil over high heat; boil for 10 to 15 minutes. Drain sausages well; grill over medium heat until browned. Shortly before serving time, place lettuce in a bowl; add just enough dressing to coat lettuce well. To serve, place sausages on buns; garnish with mustard and top with lettuce mixture. Makes 6 to 8 servings.

A fireside cookout can be as near as your own backyard!
Gather family & friends and enjoy the crisp fall air. Play touch
football, toast marshmallows, tell ghost stories, jump into
a pile of leaves...be a kid again!

Easy Reuben Stromboli

JoAnn

I love the Easy Stromboli recipe in one of our previous cookbooks. This is a whole flavorful new twist on that recipe!

1 loaf frozen bread dough, thawed
8-oz. bottle Thousand Island salad dressing, divided
1/4 lb. deli corned beef, chopped
14-1/2 oz. can sauerkraut, well drained
1/4 lb. sliced Swiss cheese
1 egg white, beaten
Optional: caraway seed

On a lightly floured surface, roll out dough into a 15-inch by 12-inch rectangle. Spread 1/3 to 1/2 cup salad dressing down the center of rectangle. Layer corned beef, sauerkraut and cheese down the center. Roll up dough, starting on one long edge; pinch ends to seal. Place seam-side down on a lightly greased baking sheet. Brush with egg white; sprinkle with caraway seed, if desired. Bake at 350 degrees for 30 to 35 minutes, until golden and cheese is melted. Slice; serve warm with remaining salad dressing. Makes 8 servings.

Whip up this super-simple veggie dip! Blend one cup cottage cheese, 1/4 cup plain Greek yogurt, one tablespoon minced onion, one teaspoon dried parsley and 1/4 teaspoon dill weed. Serve with bite-size fresh vegetables...a great go-with for sandwich suppers.

Sloppy Joe Pocket Pies

Mel Chencharick
Julian, PA

*Need something quick to take for the kids to eat after
the game? They'll love these yummy little pockets!*

2 lbs. ground beef chuck
1 onion, chopped
16-oz. can Sloppy Joe sauce
1-1/2 t. garlic powder

6 9-inch pie crusts
1 c. shredded Cheddar cheese
1 egg yolk, lightly beaten

In a large skillet, brown beef and onion over medium-high heat; drain.
Stir in sauce and garlic powder. Reduce heat to low; simmer for
20 minutes. Remove from heat; cool slightly. Meanwhile, on a lightly
floured surface, unroll pie crusts. With a 5-inch round cutter, cut
5 circles from each crust, re-rolling dough as necessary. Spoon
2 tablespoons beef mixture into the center of each circle; top with
1-1/2 teaspoons cheese. Lightly brush edges of circles with egg yolk;
fold over to enclose filling. Crimp edges with a fork to seal. Place pies
on lightly greased baking sheets. Bake at 400 degrees for 20 minutes,
or until golden. Best if served immediately. Makes 2-1/2 dozen.

Sloppy Jane Sandwiches

Joyceann Dreibelbis
Wooster, OH

*This simple slow-cooker recipe is easily doubled for
a tailgating party with friends.*

16-oz. pkg. hot dogs,
   sliced 3/4-inch thick
28-oz. can baked beans
1/3 c. chili sauce

1 t. dried, minced onion
1 t. mustard
6 to 8 hot dog buns,
   split and toasted

In a slow cooker, stir together all ingredients except buns. Cover and
cook on low setting for 2 to 3 hours. To serve, spoon into buns.
Serves 6 to 8.

Auntie B's Hamburger BBQ

Bethi Hendrickson
Danville, PA

My Aunt Barb used to make this recipe all the time when I was a kid. Now I make it for my family. It can be made ahead or even frozen for busy evenings. It is a family favorite!

1 lb. ground beef
Optional: 1/2 c. onion, chopped
1/2 c. catsup
3 to 4 T. brown sugar, packed
2 T. Worcestershire sauce

2 T. water
1 T. white vinegar
1 T. mustard
8 hamburger buns, split
Optional: 8 slices cheese

In a skillet over medium heat, brown beef with onion, if using; drain. In a small bowl, combine remaining ingredients except buns and cheese. Whisk until smooth; pour over beef mixture. Reduce heat to low; simmer for 15 to 20 minutes, stirring occasionally. Serve on hamburger buns, topped with cheese, if desired. Makes 8 servings.

Throw a pumpkin painting party. Provide acrylic paints, brushes and plenty of pumpkins...invite kids to bring their imagination and an old shirt to wear as a smock. Parents are sure to join in too!

My Famous Shredded Chicken

Vickie Zettler
Springfield, OH

I grew up in a family where my mother and grandmother made everything from scratch. Later, as a single mother raising two sons with "hollow legs," I sometimes had to invent recipes that produced not only quality but quantity. I've been making this for years, and the other day one of my sons called to ask me for the recipe. He's 43 years old now... I was so happy!

40-oz. pkg. frozen boneless,
   skinless chicken tenderloins
10-3/4 oz. can cream of
   mushroom soup
10-3/4 oz. can cream of
   chicken soup

10-3/4 oz. can cream of
   celery soup
salt and pepper to taste
8 to 10 sandwich buns, or
   cooked rice or noodles

Place chicken in a slow cooker, separating pieces. Top with soups; season with salt and pepper. Cover and cook on low setting for 8 to 10 hours, until chicken is very tender. Uncover; shred chicken with 2 forks and stir into soup mixture. Continue cooking, uncovered, for about 30 minutes, until gravy is thick. Serve chicken mixture spooned onto buns or ladled over rice or noodles. Makes 8 to 10 servings.

Give any sandwich a goblin face...the kids will love 'em!
Arrange olive slices for eyes, a banana pepper nose,
carrot crinkle ears and parsley hair.

Ultimate Grilled Cheese Sandwiches

Gladys Kielar
Whitehouse, OH

You'll never burn the grilled cheese again! This way is so much easier and more delicious. Now all of the sandwiches come out crisp and ready at the same time. You will love these.

8 slices white bread
8 slices American cheese
8 t. margarine, softened

4 t. grated Parmesan cheese,
   divided

Assemble bread and cheese to make 4 sandwiches, enclosing 2 slices cheese in each. Spread outsides of sandwiches with margarine; place on an ungreased baking sheet. Bake, uncovered, at 400 degrees for 8 minutes. Sprinkle with half of the Parmesan cheese. Flip sandwiches; sprinkle with remaining Parmesan. Return to oven for 6 to 8 minutes, until golden. Makes 4 servings.

Save the plastic liners when you toss out empty cereal boxes. They make terrific wrappers for sandwiches that will go into lunchboxes.

Becki's Turkey Salad

Rebecca Etling
Blairsville, PA

*A wonderful way to use up leftover turkey! The ingredients are
a surprising combination and taste delicious.*

4 c. cooked turkey or chicken,
  cubed
1 c. celery, chopped
3/4 c. sweetened dried
  cranberries

3/4 c. low-fat mayonnaise
2 green onions, chopped
1 t. Italian seasoning
1 t. paprika
1/2 t. pepper

Combine all ingredients in a bowl; mix with a fork until well blended.
Cover and refrigerate for one hour to allow flavors to blend. May be
served with bread as a sandwich or spooned onto lettuce as a salad.
Makes 6 to 8 servings.

Hot Turkey Sandwiches

Irene Robinson
Cincinnati, OH

*Tired of Thanksgiving leftovers? Turn them into something new and
tasty in a jiffy with these simple open-faced sandwiches.*

4 slices white bread, toasted
8 thick slices deli roast turkey

3 c. prepared stuffing
1 c. turkey gravy

Place each slice of toast on a microwave-safe plate. Divide turkey,
stuffing and gravy among toast slices. Microwave, uncovered, on
high for 30 to 40 seconds, until heated through. Makes 4 servings.

To freshen a loaf of bread that's beginning to go stale,
tuck a stalk of celery into the bread bag overnight.

Thanksgiving Sandwich

Cynthia Johnson
Verona, WI

The creamy spread in this recipe is very versatile...serve it with crackers for a tasty snack or on hot toast for breakfast.

4 English muffins, split and toasted	8 slices deli roast turkey
	Garnish: fresh spinach

Spread each English muffin half with desired amount of Orange Cream Cheese Spread. Layer 4 muffin halves each with 2 slices turkey and desired amount of spinach; top with remaining muffin halves. Makes 4 servings.

Orange Cream Cheese Spread:

8-oz. pkg. cream cheese, softened	1/2 c. sweetened dried cranberries
1/4 c. orange marmalade	1/4 c. chopped walnuts

Combine all ingredients in a bowl; mix well. Cover and refrigerate for 30 minutes before serving. Keep refrigerated.

Thanksgiving is so family-centered...why not have a post-holiday potluck with friends, the weekend after Turkey Day? Everyone can bring their favorite "leftover" concoctions and relax together.

Greek Patty Pockets

Louise Greer
Cartersville, GA

These are the tastiest hot pockets you will ever eat...all the flavors and juices cook right into the bread. My favorite will always be Greek, but Mexican is a close second. Make 'em by the dozens, as they will keep in the freezer for several months. I guarantee these will be a hit for just about any kind of fall activities you enjoy.

1 lb. ground beef, chicken
   or turkey
1/2 c. onion, finely chopped
1 T. salt
1/2 T. pepper
garlic powder and ground
   coriander to taste

6 pita rounds
Garnish: crumbled feta cheese,
   sliced black olives,
   cucumbers, lettuce and
   tomatoes, Greek salad
   dressing

Combine meat, onion and seasonings. Mix well and form into 6 patties. Slice open each pita round; place a patty inside and press closed. Wrap packets tightly in aluminum foil; freeze. To serve, place wrapped packets on a baking sheet. Bake at 350 degrees for about 25 minutes, until hot and meat is cooked through. Serve with desired toppings on the side. Makes 6 servings.

Mexican Patty Pockets:

Prepare, wrap, freeze and bake as above, using ground cumin instead of coriander and folded 8-inch corn tortillas instead of pitas. Serve with shredded Cheddar cheese, sliced black olives, lettuce and tomatoes, sour cream and salsa.

No more freezer mysteries! After wrapping, be sure to label and date food packages. A permanent ink marker works well.

82

Laurel Pizza Burgers

Debby Hardisky
New Castle, PA

This recipe was given to me by Donna Gentile, my best friend for many years. Our children attended elementary school together and loved these mini pizzas that were served in the cafeteria. All the kids couldn't wait to get one!

1 lb. ground beef
1/2 lb. bologna, ground or very finely chopped
1-1/2 c. pasteurized process cheese spread, shredded

1-1/2 c. spaghetti sauce
1 t. dried parsley
1/4 t. dried oregano
8 sandwich buns, split

Brown beef in a skillet over medium heat; drain. Stir in remaining ingredients except buns. Simmer over low heat for about 10 minutes, until cheese melts. Separate buns and arrange, cut-side up, on an ungreased baking sheet. Spoon beef mixture onto buns. Bake, uncovered, at 350 degrees for about 20 minutes, until golden. Makes 8 servings of 2 mini pizzas each.

Show your spirit...dress up a garden scarecrow
in a hometown football jersey. Go team!

Taco Sloppy Joes

Gina Wiberg
Harris, MN

I'm happy to share this recipe that our family loves. I used to make it for my family, and now our grown kids make it for their friends.

1 lb. ground beef
1/2 c. onion, chopped
10-3/4 oz. can tomato soup
2/3 c. catsup
1-1/4 oz. pkg. taco
    seasoning mix

2 T. mustard
4 to 6 hamburger buns, split
Garnish: American or
    Cheddar cheese slices
Optional: sour cream

Brown beef and onion in a skillet over medium heat; drain. Stir in soup, catsup, seasoning mix and mustard. Reduce heat to low; simmer for about 10 minutes. Add a little water if too thick. To serve, spoon onto buns. Top with cheese and sour cream, if desired. Makes 4 to 6 servings.

Pierced tin lanterns are so pretty twinkling on the dinner table... perfect for casual entertaining. Fill an empty tin can with water, freeze solid, then tap a design of holes all around with awl and hammer. After the ice has melted, set a votive candle inside.

Cheesy Quesadillas

*Shannon Reents
Loudonville, OH*

*My family loves these when we're watching football on TV.
You may wish to make some without the peppers
for those who prefer milder flavors.*

16-oz. pkg. shredded Pepper
  Jack cheese
1 c. fresh parsley, chopped

5 jalapeño peppers, seeded
  and chopped
16 8-inch flour tortillas

Combine cheese, parsley and peppers in a bowl. For each quesadilla, spoon a portion of cheese mixture into the center of a tortilla. Fold over; press the edges together. Spray a large skillet with non-stick vegetable spray; heat over medium heat. Cook quesadillas, one to 2 at a time, until golden on both sides and cheese is melted. Quesadillas may also be toasted in a toaster oven. Keep warm until serving time, or reheat in toaster oven for 5 minutes. For best results, do not reheat in a microwave. Makes 16 servings.

Whip up a zippy Tex-Mex side dish pronto! Prepare instant rice, using chicken broth instead of water. Stir in a generous dollop of spicy salsa, top with shredded cheese and cover with a lid for a few minutes, until the cheese is melted.

Chili Con Carne

Catherine Matthews
Wise, VA

A hearty, warm and spicy meal for a chilly fall evening. Top it with your favorite shredded cheese and serve with saltines.

2 lbs. ground beef
1 onion, diced
2 14-1/2 oz. cans diced
   tomatoes
2 15-1/2 oz. cans dark or
   light kidney beans

2 T. chili powder
1 T. ground cumin
2 T. salt
1 T. pepper

Brown beef and onion in a large skillet over medium heat; drain. Add undrained tomatoes and beans; mix well and stir in seasonings. Bring to a boil. Reduce heat to low and simmer for 30 minutes, stirring occasionally. Add a little water if a thinner consistency is desired. Makes 8 servings.

Host a chili cook-off! Ask neighbors to bring a pot of their "secret recipe" chili to share, then have a friendly judging for the best. You can even hand out wooden spoons, oven mitts and aprons as prizes!

Pop's Harvest Chili

Odell Underwood
Mount Hope, WV

This flavorful chili is perfect for autumn...it warms the soul and brings the family together. Serve with warm fresh-baked cornbread.

1 lb. ground beef
1/2 lb. ground pork sausage
1/4 c. green onions, chopped
1-oz. pkg. chili seasoning mix
1/2 c. yellow, red or orange
   pepper, diced

1 c. sliced mushrooms
15-1/2 oz. can Great Northern
   or pinto beans
14-1/2 oz. can lima beans
14-1/2 oz. can Italian-seasoned
   diced tomatoes

In a heavy Dutch oven over medium heat, combine beef, sausage and green onions. Sauté until browned; drain. Stir in seasoning mix, pepper, mushrooms and undrained beans and tomatoes. Simmer over low heat until vegetables are soft, about 10 minutes. Add enough water to cover ingredients, or to desired consistency. Simmer for 20 to 30 minutes, stirring occasionally. Serves 6 to 8.

October is crisp days and cool nights, a time to curl up around the dancing flames and sink into a good book.

–John Sinor

Autumn Chili Soup

Debra Collins
Gaylesville, AL

This is one of my family's favorite chili dishes during football season. Serve with corn chips.

1 lb. ground beef
14-1/2 oz. can can diced
   tomatoes
15-1/2 oz. can kidney beans,
   drained and rinsed

15-oz. can corn, drained
10-oz. can diced tomatoes and
   green chiles, drained
2 c. water
1-oz. pkg. taco seasoning mix

Brown beef in a large stockpot over medium heat; drain. Stir in undrained tomatoes and remaining ingredients; bring to a boil. Reduce heat to low. Simmer, uncovered, for 15 to 20 minutes, stirring occasionally. Makes 6 servings.

This is my favorite time of the year. We always had a big Louisiana hayride with as many adults as children coming along, singing songs and just visiting. Then after the hayride we'd all go to someone's house for a bowl of homemade chili. We still do this today on Halloween for all our grandchildren.
Fall fun doesn't get any better!

–Nan Calcagno, Grosse Tete, LA

Sent-to-Bed Tomato Soup

Margaret Welder
Madrid, IA

This soup, served with a toasted cheese sandwich, was one of my mother's favorite quick suppers. It got its name one night when I complained about having it for supper and my father sent me to bed with NO supper! I'm 75 now and I still remember that so well. I have made this soup many times for my family, and my husband still thinks it is the best.

3 T. butter
1 stalk celery, diced
1/4 c. onion, minced
2 c. canned diced tomatoes
   with juice
1/4 t. baking soda

1 t. sugar
1 T. all-purpose flour
2-1/2 c. whole milk, divided
2-1/2 t. salt, or to taste
1/4 t. pepper
Optional: minced fresh parsley

Melt butter in a saucepan over medium heat. Add celery and onion; sauté until soft. Add tomatoes with juice; bring to a boil. Add baking soda and sugar; stir down the foam. In a jar with a tight lid, shake together flour and one cup milk; add to mixture in saucepan. Stir in remaining milk, salt and pepper; return to a boil. Cook, stirring often, for about 2 minutes, until thickened. Serve soup sprinkled with parsley, if desired. Makes 6 servings.

Try something new...grilled cheese croutons! Make grilled cheese sandwiches as usual, then slice them into small squares. Toss into a bowl of creamy tomato soup...yum!

Ham & Corn Chowder

Molly Ebert
Columbus, IN

*This is a simple yet rich and comforting soup to share on a
rainy day...a delicious way to use some of that leftover holiday ham.*

2 T. butter
1/2 c. onion, finely chopped
3 T. all-purpose flour
14-1/2 oz. can chicken broth
2 c. potatoes, peeled and diced

2 15-oz. cans corn
2 c. half-and-half
1-1/2 c. cooked ham, diced
2 T. fresh parsley, snipped

Melt butter in a large saucepan over medium heat. Add onion and
cook until tender, stirring frequently. Add flour; stir to make a paste.
Slowly whisk in broth, stirring until smooth; add potatoes. Cover and
cook for 10 minutes, or until potatoes are just tender. Stir in undrained
corn and half-and-half. Reduce heat to low. Simmer, uncovered, for
6 to 8 minutes. Stir in ham and parsley; heat through but do not allow
to boil. Makes 8 servings.

Just for fun, serve up soft pretzels instead of dinner rolls...
so easy, the kids can do it! Twist strips of refrigerated bread
stick dough into pretzel shapes and place on an ungreased
baking sheet. Brush with beaten egg white, sprinkle with
coarse salt and bake as the package directs.

Simple Sweet Corn Soup

Karen Hibbert
Abergele, Wales

Fantastic for children for a warming lunchtime dish. If you prefer your onions less crunchy, sauté them in a little butter before adding to the soup. Shredded chicken can be added for a heartier soup.

2 c. chicken broth
1/2 t. garlic powder
1/4 t. dry mustard
salt and pepper to taste
1 c. frozen corn
14-3/4 oz. can creamed corn

2 green onions, chopped,
   or 2 T. dried, chopped onion
Optional: leftover mashed
   potatoes
saltine crackers

In a large saucepan over medium heat, stir together broth and seasonings. Add frozen corn, creamed corn and onions; stir again. Cook for several minutes, until corn is thawed. If a thicker soup is desired, stir in mashed potatoes to desired consistency. Bring to a boil. Reduce heat to medium-low; simmer for 20 minutes. Serve with crackers. Makes 4 servings.

When we were young, my brother Carl, sister Sue and I would go along when my parents helped my grandparents make hay. We were too little to help, but I remember fondly that Grandma would lay a blanket out in the back of the pickup. She would have a jug of lemonade, snacks and coloring books to keep us busy. In between loads of hay, we kids would nap and play outside in the small creek or near the barn. Whenever Grandpa and Dad brought in another load, we had to hop back into the truck bed and stay there until they were gone. Grandma and Mom would unload the hay into the loft. As soon as they headed out for another load, we would explore some more, catching bugs, butterflies and the occasional minnow. This is one of my favorite childhood memories.

–Sandy Groezinger, Stockton, IL

Homestyle Chicken Noodle Soup

Nancy Wise
Little Rock, AR

Simple to make...sure to make you feel better in a jiffy!
Chicken thighs are extra flavorful and budget-friendly too.
Use low-sodium broth, if you like.

1 T. oil
1 c. onion, chopped
2 c. celery, sliced
2 c. carrots, peeled and sliced
8 c. chicken broth

1-1/2 lbs. chicken thighs
7-oz. pkg. fine egg noodles,
  uncooked
salt and pepper to taste

Heat oil in a soup pot over medium heat; add vegetables. Sauté until onion is translucent, about 5 minutes; drain. Add broth to pot along with chicken, removing skin from chicken pieces, if desired. Increase heat to medium-high; bring to a boil. Reduce heat to medium-low and simmer for 30 to 45 minutes, until chicken is very tender. Remove chicken to a plate, reserving broth; let cool. Shred or dice chicken, discarding bones; set aside. Return to a boil; stir in noodles and simmer for 8 minutes. Add chicken, salt and pepper; heat through. Makes 8 servings.

For the most flavorful chicken soup, use bone-in, skin-on chicken. Skin and bones are easily removed after the chicken is cooked. Chill the soup overnight and skim off the fat before rewarming and serving your delicious soup.

Wild Rice Soup

Leona Krivda
Belle Vernon, PA

We all love this soup and it is so easy. I make it quite often, from late fall throughout winter. It's a great make-ahead, since the flavor is even better when refrigerated overnight before serving.

6-oz. pkg. long-grain &
    wild rice mix
1 T. onion, minced
2 10-3/4 oz. cans cream of
    potato soup
6 c. milk

2 c. shredded Cheddar or
    American cheese
1 T. fresh parsley, chopped
pepper to taste
1/3 to 1/2 c. crumbled bacon
    or bacon bits

Prepare rice according to package directions; transfer to a soup pot. Stir in remaining ingredients except bacon; add bacon and stir again. Simmer over medium-low heat for about 30 minutes. Cool soup to room temperature; cover and refrigerate until the next day. Shortly before serving time, reheat soup over low heat, adding a little milk if too thick. Makes 6 to 8 servings.

Start a delicious soup supper tradition on Halloween night. Soup stays simmering hot while you hand out treats, and it isn't too filling, so everyone has more room to nibble on goodies!

Cream of Potato Soup

Vickie

Simple and comforting. When I want a smoother texture, I use an immersion blender to purée it right in the saucepan.

1 T. butter
1/2 c. green onions, sliced
2 c. chicken broth
1-1/2 lbs. new yellow potatoes, cubed
salt and pepper to taste
1-1/2 c. heavy cream
Garnish: additional sliced green onions

Melt butter in a large saucepan over medium-low heat. Add green onions; cook for one minute. Add broth, potatoes and seasonings; bring to a boil over high heat. Reduce heat to low. Cover and simmer until potatoes are tender, 15 to 20 minutes. Stir in cream; heat through without boiling. Garnish soup with additional onions. Makes 4 servings.

Zucchini Bisque

Gloria Larue-Schantz
Breiningsville, PA

This recipe is delicious...our family loves it.

2 c. zucchini, chopped
1 c. water
1/2 c. tomato juice
1 T. onion, chopped
1 cube chicken bouillon
1/8 t. dried basil
8-oz. pkg. cream cheese, cubed

In a saucepan over medium heat, combine all ingredients except cream cheese. Bring to a boil; reduce heat to low. Cover and simmer for 20 minutes, or until zucchini is tender. Pour soup into a blender; add cream cheese and blend until smooth. Return to saucepan; gently heat through. Makes 4 servings.

Kitchen scissors make quick work of slicing green onions.

Lori's Green Tomato Soup

Lori Rosenberg
University Heights, OH

I made this soup last fall for the first time. When I shared it with neighbors, they gave it a thumbs-up and then went home to their own gardens in search of any lingering tomatoes to use up!

2 T. olive oil
8 slices bacon
1-1/2 c. green onions, chopped
1 T. garlic, minced
1 bay leaf
1 t. salt

1/2 t. pepper
4 to 5 c. green tomatoes, chopped
1 c. chicken broth
2 c. water

Heat oil in a large pot over medium-high heat. Add bacon; cook until nearly crisp. Add green onions, garlic and bay leaf; cook until tender. Drain; stir in salt, pepper and tomatoes. Add broth and water. Bring to a boil; reduce heat to low. Partially cover and simmer for 35 minutes. Add more salt and pepper, if needed. Discard bay leaf before serving. Serves 4.

Dress up fabric napkins in no time. Roll each napkin, tie with ribbon in russet or rich brown, and tuck a pair of acorns under the ribbon.

Mexican Soup

Carole Clark
Sterling Heights, MI

This is really the best meatless soup ever and it just takes a few minutes to put together. Make it as spicy or as mild as you like by adjusting the amounts of jalapeños and their juice.

32-oz. container chicken or
   vegetable broth
2 14-1/2 oz. cans Mexican
   stewed tomatoes, chopped
1 c. cooked rice
1/4 c. fresh cilantro, chopped

6 canned chopped jalapeños,
   drained
Optional: 3 T. jalapeño juice
Garnish: shredded Cheddar
   cheese, sour cream,
   crushed tortilla chips

Add broth and tomatoes with juice to a soup pot over medium heat. Bring to a boil; reduce heat to low. Stir in rice, cilantro, jalapeños and jalapeño juice, if using. Simmer for about 10 minutes. Ladle into bowls; garnish as desired. Serves 4.

Mom's Taco Soup

Carol McClurg
Otsego, MN

I created this slow-cooker recipe in a quest to find foods that I could enjoy with my food allergies, and that my family also liked.

1-1/2 to 2 lbs. boneless,
   skinless chicken breasts
   or tenderloins
2 to 3 c. chicken broth
24-oz. jar salsa

15-oz. can black beans
15-oz. can pinto beans
Garnish: shredded Cheddar
   cheese, sour cream,
   corn chips

Place chicken in a slow cooker; stir in broth, salsa and undrained beans. Cover and cook on low setting for 8 to 10 hours, until chicken is very tender. Shred chicken with 2 forks right in the slow cooker; stir. Serve soup with desired toppings. Serves 6 to 8.

Spinach Tortellini Soup

Pamela Bowser
Fowler, OH

*This is a family favorite passed on from one member to another.
It makes a nice meatless dish for a gathering and goes a
long way. It freezes well to keep on hand for a busy day.*

16-oz. pkg. frozen cheese
   tortellini, uncooked
1 onion, chopped
2 cloves garlic, chopped
1/4 c. olive oil
28-oz. can crushed tomatoes
28-oz. can diced tomatoes

10-oz. pkg. frozen spinach,
   thawed and squeezed dry
48-oz. can chicken broth
1 t. dried basil
salt and pepper to taste
1/2 c. grated Romano cheese

Prepare tortellini according to package directions; drain. Meanwhile,
in a soup pot over medium heat, sauté onion and garlic in oil until
transparent. Drain; add tomatoes with juice, spinach and broth.
Reduce heat to low; simmer for about 20 minutes. Add cooked
tortellini, seasonings and cheese. Simmer for 5 to 10 minutes, until
heated through. Makes 25 to 30 servings.

If you like toasted pumpkin seeds, try toasting winter squash
seeds too! Rinse seeds and pat dry, toss with olive oil to coat,
spread on a baking sheet and sprinkle with salt. Bake at
350 degrees for 10 to 15 minutes, until crisp. Enjoy as
a snack or sprinkle on hot soup for a crunchy garnish.

Beef, Barley & Spinach Soup

Alice Hardin
Antioch, CA

I love flavorful hearty soups...so good for you
and so easy to make!

3/4 lb. lean ground beef
1 c. onion, chopped
14-1/2 oz. can diced tomatoes
1-1/2 c. carrots, peeled and
   thinly sliced
1/2 c. quick-cooking barley,
   uncooked
4 c. water

1-1/2 t. beef bouillon granules
1-1/2 t. dried thyme
1 t. dried oregano
1/2 t. garlic powder
1/8 t. salt
1/4 t. pepper
6-oz. pkg. fresh baby spinach

In a soup pot over medium heat, brown beef with onion, stirring to
break up beef; drain. Stir in tomatoes with juice and remaining
ingredients except spinach; bring to a boil over high heat. Reduce heat
to low. Cover and simmer for 12 to 15 minutes, until barley and
carrots are tender, stirring occasionally. Stir in spinach; simmer
for several more minutes, until spinach starts to wilt. Makes 4 to
5 servings.

Ladle individual portions of leftover soup into small
freezer bags...seal, label and freeze. Then, when you need
a quick-fix lunch or dinner, simply transfer soup to
a microwave-safe bowl and reheat.

Easy Chicken & Dumplings

*Sharon Nunn
Mechanicsville, VA*

I created this while trying to duplicate my mother-in-law's chicken & dumplings. My family likes mine better! Delicious comfort food with very little time spent in the kitchen...my kind of recipe. I sometimes serve it over mashed potatoes. To make it healthier, I use low-sodium, low-fat soup and broth, and it's still very good. Substitute two cans of chicken breast, drained, if you're in a hurry.

1 lb. boneless, skinless chicken
  breasts
2 14-1/2 oz. cans chicken broth
2 10-3/4 oz. cans cream of
  chicken soup

Optional: 2 T. butter
12-oz. tube refrigerated
  buttermilk biscuits
dried parsley, salt and pepper
  to taste

Place chicken in a large soup pot; add enough water to cover. Bring to a boil over medium-high heat. Reduce heat to medium-low; cover and simmer for 20 minutes, or until chicken is no longer pink inside. Drain; remove chicken to a plate and cool slightly. Shred chicken with 2 forks and return to soup pot. Stir in broth, soup and seasonings. Bring to a rolling boil over medium-high heat, stirring often. Add butter for a richer flavor, if desired. Separate biscuits; tear each biscuit into 3 pieces and place on top of boiling liquid. Reduce heat to medium-low. Cover and simmer for 20 minutes, until biscuits are steamed. Makes 6 servings.

For a quick & easy table runner, choose fabric printed with autumn leaves and Indian corn in glowing gold, orange and brown. Simply pink the edges...all done!

Curry Butternut & Apple Soup

Carla Slajchert
Tampa, FL

*This soup is always a favorite of my family's when
the temperatures start to drop.*

1 butternut squash, halved
   and seeded
2 t. butter, divided
salt and pepper to taste
2 Granny Smith apples, peeled,
   halved and cored

2 c. chicken broth
1 t. garlic powder
1 t. onion powder
1 t. curry powder
1/2 c. sour cream
1 T. lime juice

Place squash halves cut-side up on a baking sheet. Add one teaspoon butter to each half; season with salt and pepper. Place apples next to squash on pan. Bake at 400 degrees for 30 to 45 minutes, until fork-tender. Scoop out squash pulp with a spoon. In a large saucepan, combine squash pulp, apples, broth and seasonings. Bring to a simmer over medium heat. Simmer for about 10 minutes, until heated through. Meanwhile, stir together sour cream and lime juice; set aside. Purée soup in batches in a blender until smooth; reheat soup, if desired. Serve in soup bowls, topped with dollops of sour cream mixture. Makes 4 to 6 servings.

When puréeing hot soup, be sure to remove the stopper from the lid of your blender so steam pressure doesn't build up inside. Cover the hole in the lid with a folded kitchen towel to prevent a mess before blending.

⬤ QUICK ⬤
Sandwiches & Soups

Best-Ever Brocco-flower Soup

*Sandy Coffey .
Cincinnati, OH*

Great for game day or for warming up after raking leaves.

3 c. broccoli, chopped
2 c. cauliflower, chopped
4 c. chicken broth
2 c. milk, divided

2 c. cooked chicken, diced
1 t. salt
6 T. cornstarch
1 c. shredded Cheddar cheese

In a large saucepan over medium-high heat, cook broccoli and cauliflower in broth until tender. Do not drain. Reduce heat to low; add 1-1/2 cups milk, chicken and salt. In a small bowl, stir cornstarch into remaining milk; mix until smooth and stir into mixture in saucepan. Cover and cook over low heat, stirring frequently, until soup is hot and thickened. Stir in cheese until melted. Makes 6 servings.

November 15 is National Clean-Out-Your-Refrigerator Day... cook up a big pot of "surprise soup" with whatever you find in the fridge! Perfect for a fall day, and the fridge will be ready for Thanksgiving groceries.

Down-East Fish Chowder

Lynda Robson
Boston, MA

Mom used to make her chowder on cold, wet days...a bowl of it always warmed us right up!

3 to 4 slices bacon
1 c. onion, chopped
3 to 4 potatoes, peeled
   and cubed
1/2 t. garlic powder
1/2 t. dried oregano

1/2 t. paprika
2 12-oz. cans evaporated milk
1 lb. cod or other white fish,
   cut into chunks
salt and pepper to taste
oyster crackers

In a Dutch oven over medium-high heat, cook bacon until crisp. Remove bacon to a paper towel, reserving drippings in pan. Add onion, potatoes and seasonings to drippings; cook and stir until onion is tender. Stir in evaporated milk; bring just to a boil. Reduce heat to low; cover and simmer for 20 minutes, stirring occasionally. Add fish; cover and simmer an additional 10 minutes, until fish flakes easily with a fork and potatoes are tender. Season with salt and pepper; garnish with crisp bacon. Serve with oyster crackers. Serves 6.

Eat-it-all bread bowls make a hearty soup extra special. Cut the tops off round bread loaves and hollow out, then rub with olive oil and garlic. Slip into the oven for 10 minutes at 400 degrees, until crusty and golden. Ladle in soup and serve right away.

Nana's Clam Chowder

Chelsea Oliver
Arlington, TN

I love clam chowder and this recipe is my favorite! My Nana makes it for me throughout the year so that I always have some of this wonderful soup whenever I want. It freezes and reheats very well.

3 slices bacon, diced
1 onion, diced
2 6-1/2 oz. cans chopped clams
12-oz. can evaporated milk

2 10-3/4 oz. cans cream of
   potato soup
2 T. lemon juice
1 T. pepper, or to taste

In a stockpot over medium heat, cook onion with bacon until onion is tender; drain. Stir in clams with juice and remaining ingredients. Bring to a boil; reduce heat to medium-low. Simmer for 10 to 15 minutes, stirring occasionally. Serves 6 to 8.

Keep the pantry stocked with canned vegetables, creamy soups, rice mixes, pasta and other handy meal-makers. If you pick up two or three items whenever they're on sale, you'll have a full pantry in no time at all.

Navy Bean Soup

MaryAlice Dobbert
King George, VA

This hearty, satisfying fall soup is ready in less than an hour, yet tastes like it simmered all day. Add a loaf of crusty French bread and this is total comfort food.

1 onion, chopped
1/2 c. butter, sliced
6 c. water
3 cubes chicken bouillon
4 c. cooked ham, shredded

1 c. instant mashed potato
  flakes
4 16-oz. cans navy beans
1 t. onion powder
1 t. garlic powder

In a Dutch oven over medium heat, sauté onion in butter until lightly golden. Stir in water and bouillon cubes; add ham and bring to a boil. Reduce heat to low; simmer for 15 minutes. Stir in instant potatoes; add beans with liquid and seasonings. Return to a boil, stirring constantly; reduce heat to low and simmer for 30 minutes. Makes 6 to 8 servings.

Dried beans are inexpensive and come in lots of varieties.
Instead of soaking, dried beans can be slow-cooked overnight
on low. Cover with water and add a teaspoon of baking soda.
In the morning, simply drain and they're ready to use.

Italian Bean & Pasta Soup

Mel Chencharick
Julian, PA

This recipe is a winner...very tasty! Get some of your friends together and have a soup & salad bar. You make the soup and have each person bring some fixin's for a salad. The ladies of our church do this and it's always a fun time for all.

2 ham hocks
12 c. water
1 onion, chopped
1 c. celery, chopped
1 c. carrots, peeled and chopped

15.8-oz. can diced tomatoes
2 16-oz. cans navy beans, drained
2 T. dried Italian seasoning
2 c. ditalini pasta, uncooked

In a large Dutch oven over high heat, combine ham hocks, water, onion, celery and carrots. Bring to a boil. Reduce heat to low and simmer, uncovered for one hour. Remove ham hocks and allow to cool. Remove meat from ham hocks, discarding skin, bones and fat. Return meat to Dutch oven; stir in tomatoes with liquid and remaining ingredients. Bring to a boil; reduce heat and simmer until pasta is tender, about 10 minutes. Serve immediately. Makes 10 to 12 servings.

Do you have a favorite soup recipe that you don't serve often due to lack of time? Try making it in a slow cooker instead! A recipe that simmers for 2 hours on the stovetop can generally cook all day on the low setting without overcooking.

Tea Room Squash Soup

Charmie Fisher
Fontana, CA

This recipe was given to me many years ago by a friend. It is such a rich and satisfying soup...perfect on a chilly autumn evening with some crusty bread! Make it lower in calories by substituting reduced-fat cheese and whole milk instead of half-and-half.

6 to 8 crookneck yellow
   squash, sliced
2 onions, chopped
1 t. garlic powder
1/2 c. butter

1/4 t. baking soda
16-oz. pkg. pasteurized process
   cheese spread, cubed
2 c. half-and-half
salt to taste

Combine squash and onions in a large saucepan; cover with water. Cook over medium heat until vegetables are fork-tender. Drain most of the liquid. Working in batches, purée mixture in a food processor until smooth; transfer to a large saucepan. Add remaining ingredients. Heat through over medium-low heat, until cheese is melted. Serve soup in small bowls. Makes 8 servings.

For a fruity cream cheese spread, combine one 8-ounce package of softened cream cheese with 1/4 cup apricot preserves. Stir until smooth. So delicious on warm slices of quick bread!

30-Minute MEALS

Ghostly Shepherd's Pie

Donna Wilson
Maryville, TN

*We have enjoyed making this cute dinner idea ever since
my older kids were little. Great for Halloween!*

1 lb. ground beef
1 onion, diced
16-oz. pkg. frozen mixed
   vegetables, divided
14-1/2 oz. can diced tomatoes
12-oz. jar beef gravy
1-1/2 c. water

2 T. butter
1/2 t. garlic powder
1/2 c. milk
2-1/4 c. instant mashed potato
   flakes
1/4 c. grated Parmesan cheese
1 egg, beaten

Brown beef and onion in a skillet over medium heat; drain. Set aside
12 peas from the mixed vegetables for the ghosts' eyes. Add
remaining mixed vegetables, tomatoes with juice and gravy to skillet.
Cook over medium heat until vegetables are tender. Meanwhile, in a
saucepan over medium heat, bring water to a boil; stir in butter and
garlic powder. Remove from heat. Stir in milk, potato flakes, Parmesan
cheese and egg. Spoon beef mixture into a lightly greased 8"x8" baking
pan. With a spoon, make 6 mounds of potato mixture on top to
resemble ghosts. Place 2 peas on each mound to resemble eyes. Bake,
uncovered, at 375 degrees for 20 minutes, or until heated through.
Serves 6.

Plan a harvest scavenger hunt for the whole family. Send them
out with a list of fall finds...a golden oak leaf, a red maple leaf,
a pumpkin, a scarecrow, a red apple and a hay bale, just to
name a few. It's not only lots of fun, it's a great way to get
outside and enjoy the fabulous fall weather!

Oktoberfest Pie

Amy Hunt
Traphill, NC

A wonderful easy meal to share after a day at the pumpkin patch.
Add some pickled beets and hot rolls on the side...your family
may just take you out for dessert!

14-oz. pkg. Kielbasa turkey
   sausage, cut into
   1/2-inch pieces
14-oz. can sauerkraut, drained
1 c. shredded Swiss cheese

3/4 c. low-fat biscuit baking mix
1/2 c. skim milk
1/2 c. non-alcoholic beer
2 eggs, beaten

Spray a 9" glass pie plate with non-stick vegetable spray. Layer
Kielbasa, sauerkraut and cheese in pie plate; set aside. In a bowl, stir
together remaining ingredients until well blended; pour over cheese.
Bake, uncovered, at 400 degrees for about 35 minutes. Let stand
several minutes; cut into wedges. Makes 6 servings.

Crunching through orange and yellow leaves on the walk
home from school...watching the Indian corn, pumpkins and
scarecrows going up on the neighbors' front porches...making a
nest under the apple tree in the backyard with a blanket and
good book to read so we could dream and soak up the chilly
fall air until we were called in for a hearty dinner of pork
chops, sweet potatoes and apple cobbler. These are my
favorite memories of autumn.

–Sheri Kohl, Wentzville, MO

One-Pot Beefy Macaroni

Robyn Binns
Crescent, IA

*This hearty dish is perfect for weeknights when you don't want
to spend the rest of the evening cleaning up the kitchen.
Everything is cooked in one pot...even the pasta!*

2 lbs. ground beef
1 onion, chopped
3 cloves garlic, chopped
3 c. water
2 14-1/2 oz. cans diced
   tomatoes

2 15-oz. cans tomato sauce
2 t. soy sauce
1 T. Italian seasoning
salt and pepper to taste
2 c. elbow macaroni,
   uncooked

Brown beef in a stockpot over medium heat; drain. Add onion and
garlic; cook for 3 to 5 minutes. Stir in water, tomatoes with juice,
tomato sauce, soy sauce and seasonings. Cook for 15 minutes, stirring
occasionally. Add uncooked macaroni. Cover and cook for 20 to
30 minutes, stirring several times. Remove from heat. Let stand,
covered, for 15 minutes. Makes 6 to 8 servings.

Need a few new ideas for family meals? Host a recipe swap!
Invite friends to bring a favorite casserole along with enough
recipe cards for each guest. While everyone enjoys a delicious
potluck, collect the recipe cards, staple together and
hand out when it's time to depart.

30-Minute
⊙ Meals ⊙

Leea's Quick Spaghetti

Leea Mercer
League City, TX

My kids love this...it's delicious and very budget-friendly too!

7-oz. pkg. spaghetti, uncooked
1 lb. ground beef
1/2 c. onion, diced
salt and pepper to taste
2 8-oz. cans tomato sauce

6-oz. can tomato paste
3 cloves garlic, minced
2 to 3 T. dried basil
1 to 2 t. dried oregano

Cook spaghetti according to package directions; drain. Meanwhile, brown beef and onion in a skillet over medium heat; drain. Add salt and pepper; stir in tomato sauce, tomato paste, garlic and seasonings. If too thick, add a little water. Reduce heat to low. Simmer for 20 to 30 minutes, stirring occasionally. Serve sauce over spaghetti. Serves 4.

Garden-Fresh Garlic Chive Bread

Gladys Kielar
Whitehouse, OH

A loaf of hot, buttery garlic bread makes any dish a meal.

1/2 c. butter, softened
1/4 c. grated Parmesan cheese
2 T. fresh chives, chopped

1 clove garlic, minced
1 loaf French bread, sliced
   1-inch thick

In a small bowl, blend butter, Parmesan cheese, chives and garlic. Spread on one side of each bread slice. Reassemble loaf; wrap in a large piece of heavy-duty aluminum foil. Seal edges, forming a packet; place on a baking sheet. Bake at 350 degrees for 20 to 25 minutes, until heated through. Makes 10 to 12 servings.

Whip up a simple rustic centerpiece... fill an old-fashioned colander with colorful apples and pears. They're perfect for snacking too.

111

Taco-Filled Peppers

Shannon Reents
Loudonville, OH

My family loves stuffed peppers and Mexican food,
so I came up with this two-in-one dish for them.

1 lb. ground beef
1-oz. pkg. taco seasoning mix
1 c. salsa
15-1/2 oz. can kidney beans,
    drained

4 peppers, tops removed
1 tomato, chopped
1/2 c. shredded Cheddar cheese
1/2 c. sour cream

Brown beef in a skillet over medium heat; drain. Stir in seasoning mix, salsa and beans; bring to a boil. Simmer for 5 minutes. Meanwhile, add peppers to a large saucepan of boiling water. Cook peppers for 3 to 5 minutes; rinse in cold water and drain well. Spoon 1/2 cup beef mixture into each pepper; arrange peppers in an ungreased 9"x9" baking pan. Cover and bake at 350 degrees for 10 to 12 minutes. Top with tomato and cheese; serve with sour cream. Makes 4 servings.

Make your own taco seasoning mix. In a jar, combine 3/4 cup dried, minced onion, 1/4 cup each salt and chili powder, 2 tablespoons each cornstarch, red pepper flakes, ground cumin and dried, minced garlic and one tablespoon dried oregano. Four tablespoons of mix equals a 1-1/4 ounce envelope.

30-Minute
☯ Meals ☯

Idaho Tacos

LaShelle Brown
Mulvane, KS

This is a tasty quick & easy meal to toss together on a busy day.
If time is short, you can bake the potatoes in the microwave while
you are making the beef mixture to go on top.

4 russet potatoes, baked
1 lb. ground beef
1-1/4 oz. pkg. taco seasoning
  mix

1/2 c. water
1 c. shredded Cheddar cheese
Garnish: sliced green onions
Optional: salsa

With a sharp knife, cut an X in the top of each warm potato; fluff pulp
with a fork and set aside. Brown beef in a skillet over medium heat;
drain. Stir in seasoning mix and water; bring to a boil. Simmer over
low heat for 5 to 7 minutes, stirring occasionally. To serve, top
potatoes with beef mixture, cheese, green onions and salsa, if desired.
Makes 4 servings.

Some of my fondest autumn memories are from the late 1950s
when our elementary school had the most fabulous Halloween
carnivals. They took place on a Saturday afternoon and all the
kids wore their costumes. Sponsored by the PTA, all our mothers
worked at the carnival and transformed the schoolyard from a
sea of concrete into a playground of all types of game booths.
They converted one of the classroom bungalows into a country
store with canned goods and scout crafts for sale. The "older"
junior high school kids came and danced to the beat of Ted
Raden (every kid took lessons at his dance studio). I remember
bringing home all kinds of junk I'd won, as well as goldfish
carried in a plastic bag filled with water. Those were
the best childhood memories!

–Debbie Muer, Encino, CA

113

Mini Turkey Pot Pies

Cathy Hillier
Salt Lake City, UT

*My kids love to help me make these little pot pies over Thanksgiving
weekend with leftovers from the big Turkey Day meal.*

1-1/2 c. cooked turkey, cubed
10-3/4 oz. can cream of chicken
  soup
1-1/2 c. frozen mixed
  vegetables, thawed

1/2 c. cooked potato, diced
12-oz. tube refrigerated
  biscuits
1/2 c. shredded Cheddar cheese

Combine chicken, soup, vegetables and potatoes in a saucepan.
Simmer over medium-low heat for 5 minutes. Meanwhile, spray
10 muffin cups with non-stick vegetable spray. Flatten biscuits
slightly; press into the bottoms and up the sides of muffin cups. Divide
chicken mixture among cups; gently press down. Top with cheese.
Bake at 350 degrees for 15 minutes, or until golden and cheese is
melted. Cool muffin tin on a wire rack for 5 minutes before removing.
Serves 4 to 6, one to 2 mini pot pies each.

Hosting dinner on Thanksgiving? Ask everyone to bring
a baby photo. Have a contest...the first person to guess
who's who gets a prize!

Barb's Chili Beans

Barbara Imler
Noblesville, IN

I created this recipe as a substitute for refried beans, but it can be served with any kind of meal, not just Mexican food. It's zingy-ier and more tasty than ordinary canned refried beans...healthier too.

1 onion, chopped
1 green pepper, chopped
1 T. butter or oil
2 15-1/2 oz. cans chili beans
10-oz. can diced tomatoes with
    green chiles, drained

1 clove garlic, minced
2 t. chili powder
1/4 t. red pepper flakes
1/2 t. salt

In a skillet over medium heat, sauté onion and green pepper in butter or oil for 5 minutes. Stir in undrained chili beans and remaining ingredients. Reduce heat to low. Simmer until thickened, about 30 minutes, stirring occasionally. Serves 4 to 6.

If you've added a bit too much hot chili seasoning,
it's easy to cool it off...simply stir in a spoonful each of
lemon juice and sugar.

Chicken Lo Mein

Stacy Lane
Millsboro, DE

I first learned this recipe in my home economics class in high school. I took it home, revamped it a little, and we've been enjoying for over ten years now! You can use any meat and vegetables you have on hand. I often share the recipe with first-time cooks and newlyweds, since it's so easy to make and easy on the budget.

1 T. oil
2 boneless, skinless chicken
   breasts, sliced
1 to 2 c. chopped broccoli,
   carrots, cabbage, celery
   and/or mushrooms
4 3-oz. pkgs. low-sodium
   chicken-flavored ramen
   noodles

4 c. water
1 T. low-sodium soy sauce
2 t. cornstarch
1 t. garlic powder
1 t. dried parsley
Optional: onion powder
   to taste

Heat oil in a large saucepan over medium heat. Add chicken; sauté until golden. Add vegetables to saucepan; break up ramen noodles and add to saucepan. In a separate saucepan, bring water to a boil. Stir in remaining ingredients, adding contents of seasoning packets to taste; add to chicken mixture. Cover and cook over medium-high heat for about 10 minutes, until vegetables are tender. Serves 5.

A notepad on the fridge is handy for a running grocery list...
no more running to the store at the last minute
before starting dinner!

Cashew Nut Chicken

LaShelle Brown
Mulvane, KS

Your family will love this easy, delicious recipe. The longer the chicken marinates, the better it will taste, so feel free to tuck it in the fridge the night before.

4 boneless, skinless chicken
    breasts, cut into 1-inch cubes
soy sauce to taste
1/2 to 1 bunch green onions,
    chopped

2 T. oil
1/2 c. cashew halves or pieces
cooked rice

Place chicken in a glass dish; add soy sauce to taste. Cover and let stand at least 15 minutes to overnight (refrigerate if more than one hour). Heat oil in a wok or skillet over medium-high heat. Drain chicken and add along with green onions; cook and stir until chicken is almost done. Add cashews; continue cooking for several minutes, until cashews soften. To serve, spoon over cooked rice. Makes 4 servings.

Stir-frying is a terrific way to make a quick and tasty dinner. Slice veggies into equal-size cubes or slices before you start cooking...they'll all be done to perfection at the same time.

Speedy Chicken-Broccoli Alfredo

Sheri West
York, SC

I came up with this recipe one night when I was short on time. My two teenagers were super hungry and needed to leave the house again quickly for the homecoming football game and the marching band that would perform at the game. It was a success!

16-oz. pkg. rotini pasta,
  uncooked
1 bunch broccoli, cut into
  flowerets
3 boneless, skinless chicken
  breasts, sliced
1 to 2 T. olive oil

10-3/4 oz. can reduced-fat
  cream of chicken soup
16-oz. jar roasted garlic
  Parmesan Alfredo sauce
1 c. shredded Italian-blend
  cheese
salt and pepper to taste

Cook pasta according to package directions, adding broccoli to cooking pot; drain. Meanwhile, heat oil in a large skillet over medium heat. Add chicken; cook until chicken juices run clear. Drain; stir in soup, sauce and cheese. Add pasta mixture; stir gently until coated with sauce. Makes 8 servings.

Olive oil stays freshest when refrigerated...pour a little
into a small squeeze bottle to keep in the cupboard
for everyday use.

Pork Cacciatore

Gladys Brehm
Quakertown, PA

This recipe was handed down in my family. It's quick and delicious.

1 T. olive oil
1 onion, chopped
4-oz. can sliced mushrooms,
   drained
1 clove garlic, minced
10-oz. can diced tomatoes

1 lb. boneless pork loin,
   cut into bite-size pieces
1 t. Italian seasoning
1/2 t. salt
1/2 t. sugar
cooked white or brown rice

Heat oil in a skillet over medium heat. Add onion, mushrooms and garlic; sauté for 3 minutes, or until slightly softened. Stir in tomatoes with juice, pork, seasonings and sugar. Cover and simmer for 10 minutes, or until pork is no longer pink in the center. To serve, spoon pork mixture over cooked rice. Serves 4 to 5.

Apple picking can be a fun family outing! The kids will be amazed to see all the different kinds of apples and so many are just the right size for little ones. Take a picnic and make a day of it, with fresh-picked apples for dessert.

Oven-Barbecued Pork Chops

Sue Neely
Greenville, IL

Need some comfort food? Try this recipe for barbecue indoors.
I like to serve it with warm cornbread and vinegary coleslaw.

3 t. canola oil, divided
4 to 6 bone-in pork chops,
   3/4-inch thick
1/4 t. salt
1/4 t. pepper

1 onion, chopped
1 clove garlic, chopped
1/3 c. orange juice
1/2 c. barbecue sauce

Heat 2 teaspoons oil in a large oven-safe skillet over high heat. Season pork chops with salt and pepper. Add to skillet and cook until almost golden; transfer to a plate. Add onion and remaining oil to skillet; cook and stir just until softened. Add garlic; cook and stir for 30 seconds. Add orange juice; cook until most of the liquid has evaporated. Stir in barbecue sauce. Return chops to the skillet, turning to coat with sauce. Place skillet in the oven. Bake, uncovered, at 400 degrees for 5 to 10 minutes, until chops are barely pink in the center. Serve chops topped with some of the sauce from the skillet. Serves 4.

Keep a few packages of frozen ravioli tucked in the freezer for speedy meals anytime. Quickly cooked and topped with your favorite sauce, they're terrific as either a side dish or a meatless main.

30-Minute ☻ **Meals** ☻

Sausage, Red Beans & Rice

Diane Cohen
Breinigsville, PA

*Looking to lighten up? This recipe is also good with
turkey sausage and light cheese.*

14-oz. pkg. smoked pork
   sausage, cut into bite-size
   pieces
10-oz. can diced tomatoes with
   green chiles
15-1/2 oz. can kidney beans,
   drained and rinsed

2 t. chili powder
2 c. water
2 c. instant rice, uncooked
1-1/2 c. pasteurized process
   cheese spread, cubed

Brown sausage in a non-stick skillet over medium-high heat for
5 minutes, stirring occasionally. Drain. Stir in undrained tomatoes,
beans, chili powder and water; bring to a boil. Stir in uncooked rice
and cheese. Reduce heat to low. Cover and simmer for 5 to 7 minutes,
until water is absorbed. Stir until cheese is completely melted.
Serves 6.

Bold Beans

Kathy Bizier-Collins
Brookfield, CT

*The first time I made this recipe, I wasn't sure if my family
would like it...these beans do have a little kick to them.
Now it's the only kind of beans they want me to make!*

16-oz. pkg. bacon, chopped
14-oz. pkg. chili-cheese smoked
   pork sausage, sliced
   1/2-inch thick

1 onion, chopped
1 green pepper, chopped
4 22-oz. cans barbecue style
   beans

In a large saucepan over medium heat, cook bacon until crisp; drain.
Add sausage, onion and pepper; cook until vegetables are tender. Stir
beans into sausage mixture. Simmer over low heat for 30 minutes,
stirring occasionally. Makes 15 to 18 servings.

Beefy Spinach Biscuit Bake

Tamatha Knauber
Lancaster, NY

Delicious...a real all-in-one meal.

2 7-oz. tubes refrigerated
　buttermilk biscuits
1-1/2 lbs. ground beef
1/2 c. onion, chopped
10-oz. pkg. frozen chopped
　spinach, thawed and drained
4-oz. can sliced mushrooms,
　drained

1 c. crumbled feta cheese or
　shredded Monterey Jack
　cheese
1/4 c. grated Parmesan cheese
1-1/2 t. garlic powder
salt and pepper to taste
2 T. butter, melted

Press and flatten biscuits into the bottom and sides of a greased
11"x7" baking pan; set aside. Brown beef and onion in a skillet over
medium heat; drain. Combine spinach and mushrooms in a bowl;
mix well. Stir in cheeses, seasonings and beef mixture. Spoon into
prepared crust. Drizzle with melted butter. Bake, uncovered, at
375 degrees for 25 to 30 minutes, until bubbly and crust is lightly
golden. Makes 6 servings.

Pinching pennies at the grocery store? Give store brands a try
for canned veggies, soups and other pantry staples. You'll find
they usually taste just as good as famous-label items...in fact,
often they're made by the same companies.

30-Minute
☾ Meals ☾

Beef Turnovers

Trisha Cooper
Spanish Fork, UT

My family loves this recipe...I double it to make sure there's enough!
For individual turnovers, cut out 6-inch circles of pie crust.

1 lb. ground beef, browned and
   drained
2 stalks celery, finely chopped
1 onion, chopped
2 cubes beef bouillon

1/8 t. pepper
1 T. soy sauce
3 T. cornstarch
1 c. cold water
2 9-inch pie crusts

Brown beef in a skillet over medium heat; drain. Add celery, onion,
bouillon, pepper and enough water to cover completely. Simmer for
10 minutes, stirring occasionally. Dissolve cornstarch in one cup
water; add to skillet and simmer until thickened. Drain, reserving
gravy from skillet. On a lightly floured surface, roll out one pie crust
into a 9-inch circle; place on a baking sheet. Spoon half of beef
mixture onto circle; fold in half and press edges with a fork. Score or
pierce 3 to 4 times to vent steam. Repeat with remaining pie crust
and beef mixture. Bake at 425 degrees until bubbly and golden, about
15 minutes. Serve reserved gravy in a gravy boat alongside
turnovers. Serves 4.

Fill vintage jelly jars with candy corn and set a tealight inside
each one. Their sweet glow will make the prettiest place settings.

123

Holiday Turkey Quesadillas

Kelly Serdynski Gray
Weston, WV

A quick-fix meal to enjoy the day after Thanksgiving or Christmas. It was inspired by my children's love of spicy Mexican food and my love of sweet & simple recipes.

4 8-inch flour tortillas
2 c. cooked turkey, shredded
1-1/2 c. whole-berry
    cranberry sauce
2 c. shredded Mexican-blend
    cheese

4 t. garlic salt, or to taste
2 t. pepper
2 t. dried tarragon
Optional: salsa verde,
    sour cream

Spray a 13"x9" baking pan generously with non-stick vegetable spray. Place 2 tortillas side-by-side in the pan. Layer turkey, sauce, cheese and seasonings equally over the tortillas. Spray remaining tortillas on both sides; place on top of ingredients in pan. Bake, uncovered, at 350 degrees for 30 to 35 minutes. Serve topped with salsa verde and sour cream, if desired. Makes 6 servings.

Bundle everyone up in their merriest mittens, hats and coats and go outdoors! While everyone's home for Thanksgiving, it's the perfect time to take photos for this year's Christmas cards.

Thanksgiving Meatballs

Stephanie Nicholson
Bobcaygeon, Ontario

Family gatherings were a special time in our home. We always celebrated with family dinners, but when I moved away after high school I didn't always make it home for Thanksgiving. This recipe came in handy when I was feeling nostalgic for that big turkey dinner!

6-oz. pkg. turkey stuffing mix   1 egg, beaten
1 lb. ground turkey   salt and pepper to taste

Prepare stuffing mix according to package directions; let cool. In a large bowl, combine turkey, egg and stuffing; season with salt and pepper. Form into 2-inch meatballs. Place in an ungreased 13"x9" baking pan. Bake, uncovered, at 350 degrees for 12 to 15 minutes, turning after 7 minutes. To serve, dip in Cranberry Spice Sauce or toss to coat. Makes one to 2 dozen meatballs.

Cranberry Spice Sauce:

1 c. water   1/4 c. orange juice
1 c. brown sugar, packed   1/2 t. allspice
12-oz. pkg. fresh cranberries   1/2 t. cinnamon
zest of 1/2 orange

In a saucepan over medium-high heat, bring water and brown sugar to a boil. Add remaining ingredients; reduce heat to low. Simmer until cranberries just start to pop and gently fall apart. Cover and chill slightly before serving. Makes 2-1/2 cups sauce.

Delicious autumn! My very soul is wedded to it.

–George Eliot

Sweet-and-Sour Pork Chops

Cheryl Culver
Perkins, OK

*Sweet-and-sour foods are a favorite with some of my family
and so I like to make this dish especially for them. It is very
good and so easy to make. Sure makes my family happy!*

20-oz. can pineapple chunks,
   drained and juice reserved
1/2 c. catsup
1 T. brown sugar, packed
1 T. cider vinegar
3 carrots, peeled and sliced
   1/4-inch thick

1 green pepper, cut into
   chunks
2 T. oil
4 to 6 pork loin chops,
   1-inch thick

In a large saucepan, combine reserved pineapple juice, catsup, brown
sugar and vinegar. Cook over medium heat for 5 minutes, until hot
and brown sugar dissolves. Add pineapple chunks, carrots and green
pepper; remove from heat. In a large skillet, heat oil over medium heat;
add pork chops and cook until golden on both sides. Arrange chops
in a lightly greased shallow 13"x9" baking pan; spread pineapple
mixture over top. Cover with aluminum foil. Bake at 350 degrees for
25 to 35 minutes, until chops are no longer pink inside and
vegetables are crisp-tender. Makes 4 to 6 servings.

A baked sweet potato is a delectable fast-fix fall side. Simply
pierce the potato several times, then bake until tender,
about 45 minutes at 400 degrees. Top with butter and
a dusting of cinnamon-sugar.

30-Minute
☻ Meals ☻

Lemon-Pepper Parmesan Chicken

Karen Hood Keeney
Bronston, KY

This is an easy-to-prepare dish I used to serve as one of the plate lunches in my deli, Karen's Konfections & Deli. My customers all loved it and I always ran out by the time lunch was over. I served it with mashed potatoes and brown gravy, green beans with bacon and a yeast roll...wonderful!

1/2 c. butter, melted
1 T. lemon-pepper seasoning
1 c. all-purpose flour
salt to taste

6 boneless, skinless chicken
  breasts
1/2 c. grated Parmesan cheese

In a shallow dish, combine melted butter and lemon-pepper seasoning. In a separate shallow dish, combine flour and salt. Dip chicken into butter mixture, then into flour mixture. Arrange chicken in a lightly greased 13"x9" baking pan. Sprinkle evenly with Parmesan cheese; drizzle with any remaining butter mixture. Cover and bake at 350 degrees for 15 minutes. Uncover; bake an additional 15 to 20 minutes, or until chicken juices run clear. Makes 6 servings.

Boneless chicken breasts are a terrific choice for speedy meals. They'll cook up even quicker if placed in a large plastic zipping bag and flattened with a meat mallet.

Easy Chicken & Tomato Rice

Shirley Howie
Foxboro, MA

I like to use rotisserie chicken in this recipe, which makes it delicious and ready to serve in a jiffy.

10-1/2 oz. can chicken broth
14-1/2 oz. can stewed tomatoes
1 t. garlic powder
1 t. dried basil

2 c. cooked chicken, cubed
1-1/2 c. instant rice, uncooked
1 c. peas

In a saucepan over high heat, combine broth, tomatoes with juice and seasonings. Bring to a boil. Add chicken, uncooked rice and peas; return to a boil. Remove from heat. Cover and let stand for 5 minutes, or until most of the liquid is absorbed. Fluff rice with a fork before serving. Serves 4.

Create mini recipe cards listing the ingredients of favorite one-dish dinners. Glue a button magnet on the back and place on the fridge...so handy whenever it's time to make out a shopping list!

30-Minute
⊙ Meals ⊙

Peppy Pizza Mac & Cheese

Sharon Haddock
Klamath Falls, OR

This recipe was shared by a lady whom I consider an excellent cook and boy, was she right...it's definitely a winner, yet so simple to make. Be prepared for lots of oohs and ahhs!

7-1/4 oz. pkg. macaroni &
   cheese mix
8-oz. can pizza sauce
30 to 40 pepperoni slices

1/2 c. shredded Monterey Jack
   cheese
1/2 c. shredded Cheddar cheese

Prepare macaroni & cheese mix according to package directions. Spread in a 13"x9" baking pan coated with non-stick vegetable spray. Spread with pizza sauce; arrange pepperoni slices on top and sprinkle with cheeses. Bake, uncovered, at 350 degrees for 30 to 35 minutes, until lightly golden and cheese is melted. Let stand 5 minutes before serving. Makes 4 servings.

American Chop Suey

Mary Ludemann
Bronx, NY

My grandmother used to make this simple dish for my mom, and Mom made it for my brother and me. I always asked her to make this for my birthday instead of something fancier! Now my two kids love it...my 8-year-old always gets excited when I make it.

16-oz. pkg. elbow macaroni,
   uncooked
1 lb. ground beef

15-oz. can tomato sauce
2 10-3/4 oz. cans tomato soup

Cook macaroni according to package directions; drain and return to cooking pot. Meanwhile, brown beef in a skillet over medium heat; drain. Add beef and remaining ingredients to macaroni. Cook over medium heat, stirring occasionally, until heated through. Serves 6.

Sophie's Parmesan-Lover's Macaroni

Jenny Bishoff
Mountain Lake Park, MD

This dish was my daughter's first effort at homemade macaroni & cheese. We changed it up to suit her dad's favorite flavors for a special Fathers' Day meal. He loved it, and if you love fresh Parmesan and garlic, you will too! Use rotini pasta if you like.

16-oz. pkg. elbow macaroni, uncooked
1/4 c. butter, sliced
1/4 c. all-purpose flour

2 c. milk
2 to 4 cloves garlic, minced
1 c. shredded Parmesan cheese
salt and pepper to taste

Cook macaroni according to package directions; drain. Meanwhile, melt butter in a medium saucepan over medium heat. Whisk in flour until a smooth paste is formed; cook and stir constantly for one minute. Slowly stir in milk and garlic. Increase heat slightly. Cook, stirring constantly, until mixture boils and thickens to desired consistency. Add cheese, salt and pepper. Stir until cheese is melted; pour over macaroni and stir well. Makes 6 to 8 servings.

A range of cooking times is often given on packages of pasta. The first cooking time is for al dente (firm to the bite) and the second cooking time is for a softer pasta. You choose!

My Favorite Rice Pilaf

Shirley Howie
Foxboro, MA

This pilaf is delicious served alongside any kind of meat or fish, or even on its own. Very versatile and flavorful! I have been making this for years now and it is my go-to recipe for rice.

2 t. butter
1/2 c. onion, chopped
1/2 c. celery, chopped
1-1/2 c. long-cooking rice,
   uncooked

4 c. hot water
2-1/2 oz. pkg. chicken noodle
   soup mix
1/2 t. dried thyme
1/2 t. dried sage

Melt butter in a large skillet over medium heat. Add onion and celery; sauté until tender. Add rice; cook and stir until lightly golden. Add hot water and soup mix; stir well. Bring to a boil. Reduce heat to low; stir in herbs. Cover and cook for 20 minutes, or until liquid is absorbed, stirring often. Makes 6 servings.

It's not hard to get more veggies into your family's meals. Keep frozen vegetables on hand to toss into favorite pasta or rice dishes...they'll blend right in!

Spicy-Sweet Broccoli

Lisa Ann Panzino DiNunzio
Vineland, NJ

One of my family's favorite side dishes. It's sweet and spicy
all in one...we love it!

2 bunches broccoli, cut
   into flowerets
2 T. cider vinegar
2 T. light brown sugar, packed
1/2 t. red pepper flakes

2 T. extra-virgin olive oil
2 cloves garlic, pressed
4 long strips lemon zest
2 T. butter
1/2 t. sea salt

In a large saucepan, bring one inch of water to a boil over high heat.
Add broccoli. Reduce heat to medium; cover and cook for 5 minutes,
or until fork-tender. Drain and set aside in a large serving bowl; cover
to keep warm. In a small bowl, whisk together vinegar, brown sugar
and red pepper flakes; set aside. In a large skillet, heat olive oil over
medium-high heat. Add garlic and lemon zest to skillet; cook for
30 seconds, or until garlic turns lightly golden. Discard zest. Stir in
butter until melted; add vinegar mixture and salt. Stir and remove
from heat. Pour hot vinegar mixture over steamed broccoli; toss to
coat. Adjust seasoning and drizzle with a little more oil, if desired.
Serves 6 to 8.

An oh-so-simple harvest decoration...roll out a wheelbarrow
and heap it full of large, colorful squash and pumpkins.

30-Minute
☉ Meals ☉

Zucchini Nuggets

Christina Davis
Smithfield, VA

This recipe is special because Mom made these with the zucchini from our family garden while we were growing up. It was one sure way to get us to eat our veggies...there were never any leftovers. We still make them today and now our kids love them!

1 c. zucchini, grated
1 onion, grated
3/4 c. all-purpose flour
1 t. dried parsley

2 eggs, beaten
1/2 c. grated Parmesan cheese
oil for frying

In a bowl, mix together all ingredients except oil. Heat oil in a skillet over medium heat. Add batter by tablespoonfuls. Cook until golden on both sides. Serves 4 to 5.

Zesty Mustard Sauce

Irene Robinson
Cincinnati, OH

Delicious on hot steamed broccoli, asparagus spears or green beans.

3/4 c. mayonnaise
3 T. lemon juice

1-1/2 T. Dijon mustard
1/2 c. heavy cream

In a bowl, mix together mayonnaise, lemon juice and mustard; set aside. In a separate bowl, with an electric mixer on high speed, beat cream until soft peaks form. Fold whipped cream into mayonnaise mixture. Keep refrigerated. Makes about 2 cups.

Create a trail of glowing pumpkins in no time...after carving, tuck a string of outdoor-safe battery-operated lights inside each pumpkin.

Stir-Fried Squash Medley

Ramona Wysong
Barlow, KY

I came up with this tasty recipe years ago, when I wanted to make use of some extra yellow squash and zucchini. It was a hit!

2 T. olive oil
2 c. zucchini, sliced
2 c. yellow squash, sliced
1/2 c. onion, chopped

1 c. tomatoes, diced
1 t. salt
pepper to taste
Optional: 1/4 c. chicken broth

Add olive oil to a wok or large skillet. Heat over medium-high heat for 2 minutes. Add zucchini, squash and onion; cook and stir for 2 minutes. Add tomatoes, salt and pepper. Reduce heat to medium-low. Simmer for 8 to 10 minutes, until vegetables are crisp-tender, stirring occasionally. Add broth if mixture becomes too dry. Makes 4 to 6 servings.

Fall has always been my favorite time of year. I grew up in the suburbs in the 1950s, when burning leaves in the street was still allowed. It was my job to help Dad rake leaves. It took a few hours to rake everything to the front yard and into the street. When we piled our leaves high, Dad would toss that match and they would begin to burn and it smelled so good. It wasn't quite fall until I went into the house and grabbed two potatoes that Dad would place in those burning leaves to roast. When the leaves were burned, our potatoes were done. They were the best potatoes I ever tasted and it was a special time that my Dad and I shared.

– Arden Regnier, East Moriches, NY

30-Minute
○ Meals ○

Braised Beans & Tomatoes

Gail Peterson
Stockton, KS

*I love this recipe! In the summer I use fresh-from-the-garden
ingredients. Once my garden is tucked away for the year, then what
I have frozen or canned is perfect for this recipe.*

2 T. butter
1 onion, thinly sliced
3 cloves garlic, minced
16-oz. pkg. frozen cut
   green beans

14-1/2 oz. can diced tomatoes,
   drained
1 to 1-1/2 c. chicken broth
salt and pepper to taste

Melt butter in a large skillet over medium heat; sauté onion. Add
garlic, beans, tomatoes and enough broth to cover everything.
Increase heat to high; bring to a boil. Reduce heat to low; cover and
simmer for 5 to 10 minutes, until beans are tender. Uncover; simmer
for 5 minutes. Season with salt and pepper. Serves 6.

Make crispy potato pancakes with leftover mashed potatoes.
Stir an egg yolk and a little minced onion into 2 cups cold
mashed potatoes. Form into patties; dust with a little flour and
pan-fry in a little oil until golden. Serve with sour cream
for a delicious treat.

135

Honey-Glazed Carrots & Pecans

Paulette Alexander
Saint George's, Newfoundland

Even finicky eaters like my husband enjoy this side dish. It goes so nicely with practically any meat or fish.

1/3 c. pecans, coarsely chopped
2 T. canola oil, divided
3/8 t. salt, divided
1 T. butter
2 lbs. carrots, peeled, halved
    lengthwise and sliced

1/2 t. chili powder
2 T. honey
salt and pepper to taste

On a rimmed baking sheet, toss pecans with one tablespoon oil and 1/8 teaspoon salt. Toast at 375 degrees for about 5 minutes; set aside. In a large non-stick skillet over medium-high heat, melt butter with remaining oil. Add carrots; reduce heat to medium. Cover; cook for 12 minutes, stirring occasionally. Stir in chili powder and remaining salt. Cover; cook until tender, about one minute. Remove from heat. Stir in honey; season with salt and pepper. Serve carrots with pecans sprinkled on top. Serves 4 to 6.

Sweet Bacon & Brussels

Amy Hunt
Traphill, NC

My niece's mother-in-law Paulette shared this delicious and simple recipe with me. It's a great side dish with any meal.

6 slices bacon
1/2 to 3/4 lb. Brussels sprouts,
    trimmed

6 T. brown sugar, packed

In a skillet over medium heat, cook bacon until crisp. Remove bacon to a paper towel, reserving drippings. Cut any larger Brussels sprouts in half. Add sprouts to drippings; sprinkle with brown sugar. Sauté until tender, 6 to 10 minutes; drain. Transfer sprouts to a serving dish; toss with crumbled bacon. Serves 4.

Fried Peppered Cabbage

Irene Robinson
Cincinnati, OH

This simple dish is delicious with pork chops.

1/4 c. butter, sliced
1 head cabbage, coarsely
    chopped

salt and pepper to taste
3 T. sour cream

Melt butter in a large skillet over high heat; add cabbage. Sauté, stirring constantly, for about 2 minutes, until tender-crisp but not wilted. Season with salt and a very generous amount of pepper. Stir in sour cream. Serve immediately. Makes 6 servings.

When I was growing up in Saint Anthony, Idaho, during the 1960s and 1970s, school was let out for a week in October so the farmers could harvest potatoes. If you were old enough, you could get a job riding on the picker and sorting out the leaves and plants from the potatoes. What a dirty job, but so much fun! And the potato dishes were abundant.

—Lisa Seckora, Bloomer, WI

Pan-Roasted Fingerling Potatoes

Krista Marshall
Fort Wayne, IN

We are tater lovin' people. I'm always looking for new ways to prepare them, and these buttery-tasting little potatoes are the perfect side dish to any meal.

1 lb. yellow fingerling potatoes	1 t. dried rosemary
2 T. olive oil	1 t. dried thyme
2 cloves garlic, minced	salt and pepper to taste
2 t. dried parsley	Garnish: additional parsley

Cut any larger potatoes in half. In a Dutch oven or deep skillet, cover potatoes with cold water. Bring to a boil over medium-high heat. Cook until just fork-tender, about 5 to 7 minutes; drain well and set aside. Wipe out pan with a paper towel. Add oil; heat over medium-high heat. Add potatoes and seasonings; stir to combine. Sauté until golden on all sides, stirring often, about 10 to 15 minutes. Garnish with a sprinkle of parsley. Makes 4 servings.

Pick up some paper plates and cups in seasonal designs... they'll make dinner fun when you're in a hurry and clean-up will be a breeze.

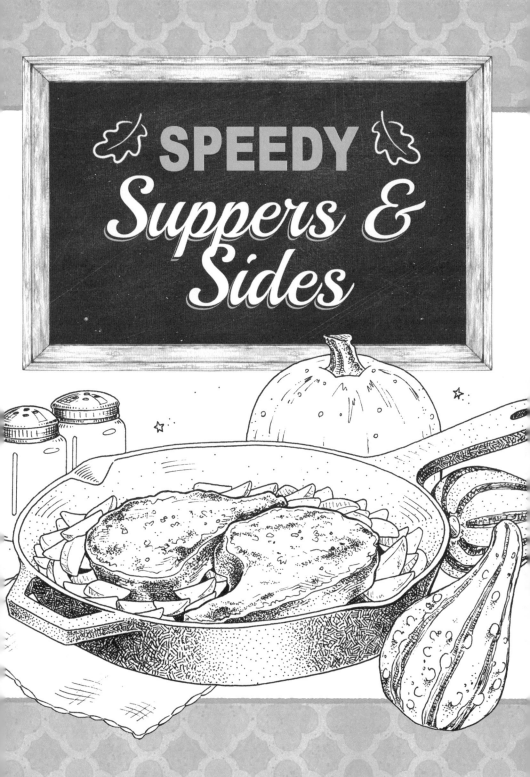

SPEEDY
Suppers & Sides

Millie's Pepper Steak

Rosemary Hart
Carol Stream, IL

I have so many fond memories of my mother in the kitchen. I remember coming home from school and Mom making this for dinner. She and I would talk about our day while she cooked. This recipe takes me back... it is even tastier the next day!

1 lb. beef sirloin, flank or
    round steak, thinly sliced
1/2 c. all-purpose flour
1 to 2 T. oil
2 cloves garlic, chopped
garlic powder, salt and pepper
    to taste

1 t. dried oregano
1 t. browning and seasoning
    sauce
1 green pepper, sliced
3/4 c. canned diced tomatoes
1 onion, chopped
cooked rice

Dredge beef in flour; set aside. Heat oil in a skillet over medium-high heat. Add beef and cook until browned. Drain; add enough water to cover beef. Stir in garlic, seasonings and sauce; bring to a boil. Reduce heat to low; cover and cook for 30 minutes. Add tomatoes and green pepper; cook an additional 15 minutes, or until beef is tender. Serve over cooked rice. Makes 4 servings.

Let the kids help with meals! Younger children can
scrub vegetables and tear salad greens. Older kids can measure,
chop, stir and take part in meal planning and shopping.
Give 'em a chance...they may just surprise you!

❁ SPEEDY ❁
Suppers & Sides

Comfort Chicken Casserole

Vicki Meredith
Grandview, IN

My mother made this recipe often with leftover chicken or turkey.
It's so easy...you don't even need to cook the noodles first.

10-3/4 oz. can cream of
   mushroom soup
1/2 c. milk
1 c. cooked chicken or turkey,
   cubed
1 c. shredded Cheddar cheese

1/2 c. onion, diced
8-oz. pkg. egg noodles,
   uncooked
1 c. water
1/4 c. soft bread crumbs

In an ungreased 2-quart casserole dish, stir together soup and milk.
Add chicken, cheese and onion; mix well. Stir in uncooked noodles;
pour water over all. Sprinkle with bread crumbs. Bake, uncovered, at
350 degrees for about 50 minutes, or until golden. Serves 4.

At Halloween, my parents made sure that there was plenty of
scary fun to be had for us kids! We'd all go out to a local
pumpkin patch and pick out four of the best-looking pumpkins
to bring home for my dad to carve. The excitement would build
in my mind...Halloween! Mom helped us plan our costumes,
while my sister Michele and I "helped" her in the kitchen as she
created delicious goodies...crispy treat pumpkins, monster toes,
popcorn and caramel apples. Oh, the smells just made me so
excited! On the big night, as Michele and I dressed up, Dad
would greet the trick-or-treaters with his sinister laugh and
recordings of scary sounds. By the time we returned home, our
pillowcases (and tummies) were filled to the brim with candy
and our hearts were happy for another magical Halloween!

–Melissa Fialer, Palo Alto, CA

141

Simple Ginger Chicken

Kathy Courington
Canton, GA

My daughter's girlfriend says this is the best chicken she has ever had. A friend shared the recipe with me years ago...every time I serve it, it disappears! It really is that simple and that good.

6 to 8 chicken thighs
1/2 to 1 onion, chopped
1 c. low-sodium soy sauce

1 c. water
3 T. ground ginger, or to taste
cooked rice

Combine all ingredients except rice in a Dutch oven. Bring to a boil over medium high heat; reduce heat to low. Cover and simmer for one hour, or until chicken juices run clear. Check occasionally, adding more water as needed. May also be cooked in a slow cooker on low setting for 6 to 8 hours. Serve over cooked rice. Serves 6 to 8.

Sunday Chicken

JoAlice Patterson-Welton
Lawrenceville, GA

This is an easy chicken dish for a busy week. So delicious and moist...a family favorite!

5 to 6 boneless, skinless
chicken breasts
1/2 c. sour cream

1/4 c. soy sauce
10-1/2 oz. can French onion
soup

Arrange chicken in a 13"x9" baking pan coated with non-stick vegetable spray; set aside. Combine remaining ingredients in a saucepan. Cook and stir over low heat just until well blended; spoon over chicken. Cover and bake at 350 degrees for 55 minutes, or until chicken juices run clear. Serves 5 to 6.

Fresh vegetables will stay bright-colored and tasty if you add a tablespoon or two of vinegar to the water when boiling or steaming.

✿ SPEEDY ✿
Suppers & Sides

Hot Cherry Pepper Chicken
Mariann Raftery
Scarsdale, NY

Long and slow is the way to go with this flavorful dish! For adults I use the whole jar of peppers, because they love the hot spicy taste. I use fewer peppers when cooking for children.

1 T. olive oil
1 onion, sliced
4 to 6 cloves garlic, chopped
salt and pepper to taste

12 chicken drumsticks, thighs
and wings
32-oz. jar hot cherry peppers,
divided

In an ungreased deep 13"x9" baking pan, combine oil, onion, garlic, salt and pepper; stir to mix. Add chicken; toss together well. Pour 1/2 jar of cherry peppers with juice over chicken. Bake, uncovered, at 325 degrees for 45 minutes; turn chicken over. If desired, for a very spicy dish, pour remaining peppers and juice over chicken. Cook, uncovered, another 60 minutes, or until chicken juices run clear, turning chicken over several times. Serves 6 to 8.

Polynesian Chicken
Leslie Kirzner
Ramsey, NJ

This is quick and delicious. I concocted it one night with pantry ingredients when we were creating a "Tiki Night" for my husband's birthday, complete with decorations and coconut drinks.

4 chicken breasts
1 c. teriyaki marinade
8-oz. can crushed pineapple

8-oz. can whole-berry cranberry
sauce

Combine chicken and marinade in a large plastic zipping bag; seal bag. Refrigerate for several hours, turning bag once or twice. Drain, discarding marinade. Place chicken in a greased 13"x9" baking pan. Pour pineapple with juice and cranberry sauce over chicken. Bake, uncovered, at 350 degrees for one hour, or until chicken is golden and juices run clear. Makes 4 servings.

Pork & Pepper Stir-Fry

Dale Duncan
Waterloo, IA

This delicious one-dish dinner cooks up in a jiffy. Boneless pork chops may be used instead of pork tenderloin.

1 T. olive oil
1-lb. pork tenderloin, thinly
  sliced
2 green or yellow peppers,
  thinly sliced
1/2 c. orange juice

2 T. soy sauce
1 T. honey
1 T. cornstarch
1/2 t. ground ginger
cooked rice
Optional: chow mein noodles

Heat oil in a large skillet over medium-high heat. Add pork; cook and stir for 4 minutes, until pork is no longer pink. Add peppers; cook and stir another 4 minutes, or until peppers are crisp-tender. In a small bowl, combine remaining ingredients except rice and noodles; mix well and add to skillet. Bring to a boil. Cook and stir until sauce thickens, one to 2 minutes. Serve over cooked rice, garnished with chow mein noodles, if desired. Makes 4 servings.

Start a Thanksgiving tradition. Before dinner, take time to hold hands and ask everyone at the table to share what they're thankful for...some of the sweetest memories will be made.

❀ SPEEDY ❀
Suppers & Sides

Bacon & Apple Pork Chops

Becky Drees
Pittsfield, MA

Tart-sweet apples, caramelized onion, salty bacon...
all the savory flavors of autumn at its best!

6 boneless pork chops
garlic powder, salt and pepper
   to taste
2 T. olive oil
3 thick-cut slices bacon, diced

1/2 c. onion, diced
1 to 2 cloves garlic, minced
2 apples, peeled, cored and
   diced
Garnish: honey

Sprinkle pork chops on both sides with seasonings; set aside. Heat oil
in a cast-iron skillet over medium-high heat. Add chops; cook just
until browned on both sides. Reduce heat to medium-low. Cover and
cook until chops are no longer pink in the center; do not overcook.
Meanwhile, in a separate skillet over medium heat, cook bacon until
crisp. Push bacon to one side of the skillet. Add onion and garlic to
the other side; cook until onion starts to soften. Add apples; stir
contents of skillet together. Simmer for about 10 minutes, until apples
are soft, reducing heat if necessary. To serve, spoon apple mixture
over chops; drizzle with a small amount of honey. Serves 6.

A cast-iron skillet is wonderful for cooking up homestyle
dinners. If it hasn't been used in awhile, season it first.
Rub it lightly with oil, bake at 300 degrees for an hour and
let it cool completely in the oven. Now it's ready
for many more years of good cooking!

145

Baked BBQ Ranch Turkey Tacos

Marie Matter
Dallas, TX

*Barbecue meets Tex-Mex for these delicious tacos! Baking the
tacos allows the cheese to melt and the shells to crisp
up perfectly. Your family will go wild over these!*

1 T. olive oil
1 lb. ground turkey
2 T. ranch salad dressing mix
1-1/2 c. barbecue sauce

6 crisp corn taco shells
2 c. shredded sharp Cheddar
  cheese
Garnish: diced avocado

In a large skillet, heat oil over medium-high heat. Add turkey and
cook just until golden, breaking it up with a spatula. Stir in dressing
mix and barbecue sauce. Reduce heat to medium-low; cook and stir
for 3 to 4 minutes. Stand up taco shells in an ungreased 8"x8" baking
pan. Divide turkey mixture among taco shells; sprinkle with cheese.
Bake, uncovered, at 400 degrees for 10 minutes, or until cheese
melts. At serving time, garnish with avocado. Makes 6 servings.

Do you have lots of kids coming over for an after-game party?
Make it easy with do-it-yourself tacos or mini pizzas...guests can
add their own favorite toppings. Round out the menu with
pitchers of soft drinks and a delicious dessert. Simple and fun!

Quick Tamale Pie

Julie De Fusco
Henderson, NV

When a friend of mine shared this with me, I fell in love with it. It's perfect when guests pop in, as most of the ingredients are already in the pantry. It also freezes well if there are leftovers. Save time by using a box of cornbread mix...just follow the package instructions.

1 lb. ground beef or turkey
Optional: 1 onion, chopped
14-1/2 oz. can Mexican or
    Italian-seasoned stewed
    tomatoes
1-1/4 oz. pkg. taco seasoning
    mix

11-oz. can corn, drained
4-oz. can chopped black olives,
    drained
3/4 c. water

In a large oven-safe skillet over medium heat, brown beef with onion, if using; drain. Stir in tomatoes with juice and remaining ingredients. Reduce heat to low and simmer, uncovered, for several minutes, until liquid is reduced. If not using an oven-proof skillet, transfer mixture to a greased 11"x9" baking pan. Pour Cornbread Topping batter over top. Bake, uncovered, at 400 degrees for about 25 minutes, until topping is golden and tests clean with a knife tip. Serves 8.

Cornbread Topping:

1 c. milk
1/4 c. oil
1 egg, beaten
1 c. cornmeal

1 c. all-purpose flour
1 T. baking powder
Optional: 2 T. sugar

Stir together all ingredients until smooth.

Dust off Mom's vintage casserole dishes...they're just right for baking family-pleasing hearty casseroles, with a side dish of sweet memories.

Easy Chicken Manicotti

Becky Holsinger
Belpre, OH

Although I love to cook, I don't claim to be all that great at it. I was given this recipe when I got married and not only is it easy, it tastes great! I know when I make this dish it will be good, no matter what.

26-oz. jar pasta sauce
1/2 c. water
10 boneless, skinless chicken
   tenders
1 t. garlic salt
1/2 t. Italian seasoning

10 manicotti pasta shells,
   uncooked
2 c. shredded mozzarella cheese
Optional: chopped fresh basil
   and oregano

In a bowl, mix pasta sauce and water. Spread 1/3 of sauce mixture in an ungreased 13"x9" inch glass baking pan; set aside. Sprinkle chicken with seasonings. Insert one chicken tender into each uncooked manicotti shell, stuffing from each end, if necessary. Arrange shells over sauce mixture in baking pan. Pour remaining sauce mixture evenly over shells, covering completely. Cover with aluminum foil. Bake at 350 degrees for about an hour, until shells are tender and chicken is no longer pink in the center. Top with cheese. Bake, uncovered, for 5 minutes, or until cheese is melted. Garnish with herbs, if desired. Serves 5 to 7.

Whip up some herb butter to go with hot rolls. Blend 1/2 cup softened butter, one tablespoon chopped fresh parsley, 1-1/2 teaspoons minced garlic, one teaspoon Italian seasoning and a squirt of lemon juice. Wrap well and refrigerate or freeze.

Roasted Veggies & Penne Pasta
Ramona Wysong
Barlow, KY

This recipe is great for getting everyone to eat more vegetables! You can vary the veggies with your favorites...I like to use different kinds of peppers from the farmers' market. Sometimes I add more cheese too, since my family likes cheesy dishes. Enjoy!

16-oz. pkg. penne pasta, uncooked
2 zucchini, quartered lengthwise and sliced 1-inch thick
2 yellow squash, quartered lengthwise and sliced 1-inch thick
2 red peppers, cut into 1-inch squares
1 onion, cut into 1-inch squares
1 to 2 T. olive oil
kosher salt to taste
3 c. shredded mozzarella cheese, divided
1/4 c. plus 2 T. grated Parmesan cheese, divided

Cook pasta according to package directions, just until tender; drain. Meanwhile, combine vegetables in a greased 13"x9" baking pan. Drizzle with oil and season with salt. Bake, uncovered, at 425 degrees for 15 to 20 minutes, stirring once or twice, until golden and caramelized. Add cooked pasta to vegetable mixture along with 2 cups mozzarella cheese and 1/4 cup Parmesan cheese. Toss to mix well. Sprinkle with remaining cheeses. Return to oven for 5 minutes, or until cheese melts. Makes 6 to 8 servings.

Cut the corner from a paper envelope, then snip off the tip to create a tiny funnel perfect for filling salt & pepper shakers.

Deviled Turkey Drumsticks

Teri Lindquist
Gurnee, IL

*We love these big flavorful drumsticks! Not only are they fun to eat,
they are budget-friendly and a wonderful surprise anytime.*

6 turkey drumsticks
1/4 c. oil
1 T. Worcestershire sauce
2 shakes hot pepper sauce,
   or to taste

1/2 t. garlic powder
1/2 t. onion powder
1/4 t. paprika
1 t. salt
1/2 t. pepper

Place drumsticks in an aluminum foil-lined roasting pan. In a small
bowl, whisk together remaining ingredients; brush evenly over
drumsticks. Bake, uncovered, at 400 degrees for 1-1/4 to 1-1/2 hours,
until drumsticks are golden and no longer pink inside. Baste
occasionally with pan drippings. Remove from oven; let stand
5 minutes. For easier handling, wrap a strip of foil around the end
of each drumstick. Makes 6 servings.

For my daughters Lynda and Elaine and me, fall always signaled
back-to-school time. I was secretary at our local high school for
27 years, so we shared this special time. Buying new fall clothes
and school supplies was the highlight of our year. My daughters
helped get the school ready, putting up fresh fall and sports-
themed bulletin boards. Everywhere there was that special smell
of new clothes, brand spankin' new notebooks and school buses
being prepped for the first day of school. Even now, after being
retired for 15 years, I still feel nostalgic when I see the buses
starting to roll and the students waving, as I remember my own
sweet daughters and the first day of school.

–Bunny Palmertree, Carrollton, MS

❀ SPEEDY ❀
Suppers & Sides

Tasty Dijon Pork Chops

Sue Klapper
Muskego, WI

My mother-in-law was a good but unadventurous cook, so my husband was a little afraid when I tried new recipes as a newlywed. After tasting these delicious pork chops, he learned to enjoy my experiments. Thirty years later, we still love them!

2 T. Dijon mustard
2 T. Italian salad dressing
1/4 t. pepper

4 boneless pork chops
1 onion, sliced

Combine mustard, salad dressing and pepper in a small bowl. Brush over both sides of pork chops; reserve any extra mustard mixture. Add chops in a skillet sprayed with non-stick vegetable spray. Cook, covered, over medium heat for about 30 minutes. Turn chops and baste occasionally with mustard mixture; add a little water if needed. Add onion during last 5 minutes. Makes 4 servings.

Perfect Pork Chops

Cris Goode
Mooresville, IN

This is simply the easiest and best way I have found to make a good pork chop. My family adores our Pork Chop Night and guests always rave about it!

4 to 6 center-cut pork chops   seasoned salt to taste

Preheat broiler and broiler pan. Season pork chops on one side with seasoned salt. Place on hot broiler pan; season other side. Broil for 5 minutes, or until browned. Turn; insert a meat thermometer into a chop. Broil until internal temperature reaches 145 degrees. Remove chops to a platter; let stand for 3 minutes. Makes 4 to 6 servings.

Ready, set, cook! When pasta is on the menu, put a big pot of water on the stove as soon as you get home. Dinner will be ready in a jiffy!

Sue's Hamburger Pie Deluxe

Susan Whitson
Telford, TN

As a newlywed, I made this for my parents, who said it was a keeper! It tastes like the great hamburgers you remember as a kid. Add some French fries and a crisp salad for an easy hearty meal that everyone loves.

9-inch pie crust
1-1/2 to 2 lbs. ground beef
1 onion, finely chopped
1 green pepper, finely chopped
1 c. all-purpose flour
1/2 c. milk
1 c. shredded Cheddar cheese
1/2 to 1 c. sweet pickle relish

1/4 c. catsup
1/4 c. mustard
dried oregano, salt and pepper
    to taste
Optional: additional cheese
Garnish: catsup, mustard, sliced
    dill pickles and tomatoes

Place pie crust in a 9" deep-dish pie plate sprayed with non-stick vegetable spray. Bake at 350 degrees for 15 minutes, or until golden; cool. Meanwhile, brown beef in a skillet over medium heat. Add onion and pepper when beef is half-done; cook until tender and drain. Sprinkle with flour and toss to coat; stir in milk. Mixture will be sticky. Remove from heat. Add remaining ingredients except optional cheese and garnish. Mix well; spoon into crust. Bake, uncovered, at 350 degrees for 30 minutes. Top with additional cheese during the last 5 minutes, if desired. Let stand for 10 minutes. Cut into wedges; garnish as desired. Makes 6 servings.

Pitch a tent in the backyard on a fall night so the kids can camp out, tell ghost stories and play flashlight tag. What a great way to make memories!

Veggie Spaghetti Pie

Mary Donaldson
Enterprise, AL

To please my vegetarian guests, I made my favorite spaghetti pie minus the pepperoni slices I usually include. My guests loved it and asked for the recipe.

7-oz. pkg. spaghetti, uncooked
3 T. butter, softened and divided
1 egg, beaten
1 c. grated Parmesan cheese, divided
1/2 c. small-curd cottage cheese

1 onion, chopped
1 yellow pepper, chopped
6-oz. jar artichoke hearts, drained and chopped
4-oz. can sliced portabella mushrooms, drained

Cook spaghetti according to package directions, just until tender; drain. Stir in 2 tablespoons butter, egg and 1/2 cup Parmesan cheese. Press mixture into a 10" pie plate coated with non-stick vegetable spray. Spread cottage cheese over spaghetti mixture; set aside. In a skillet over medium heat, cook onion and yellow pepper in remaining butter until soft. Add artichokes and mushrooms; mix well. Spoon vegetable mixture over cottage cheese; top with remaining Parmesan cheese. Bake, uncovered, at 350 degrees for 25 to 30 minutes, until golden and heated through. Let stand 5 minutes before cutting. Makes 6 to 8 servings.

Create a meal plan for the week, including all of your favorite quick & easy meals...spaghetti on Monday, chicken pot pie on Tuesday and so forth. Post it on the fridge along with a shopping list...making dinner will be a snap!

Cream Cheese-Stuffed Chicken

Paulette Alexander
Saint George's, Newfoundland

One of our favorite meals! It's so easy to make and leaves everybody quite satisfied. I sometimes make it when cooking as a volunteer with elementary children at our local school.

4 boneless, skinless chicken
  breasts
1/2 c. cream cheese with chives,
  softened
4 T. butter, softened and divided

1/2 c. brown sugar, packed
1/4 c. mustard
4 wooden toothpicks, soaked
  in water
Optional: cooked rice

Place each chicken breast between 2 pieces of plastic wrap. Pound to 1/4-inch thick and set aside. In a small bowl, beat cream cheese and 2 tablespoons butter to a creamy consistency. Blend in brown sugar and mustard. Divide mixture among chicken breasts; spread evenly. Fold chicken over; fasten with toothpicks. Place chicken in a single layer in a lightly greased 9"x9" baking pan. Melt remaining butter and drizzle over chicken. Bake, uncovered, at 350 degrees for 25 to 30 minutes, until chicken juices run clear. Discard toothpicks. Serve with cooked rice, if desired. Makes 4 servings.

A quick fall craft for kids...hot glue large acorn caps onto round magnets for whimsical fridge magnets.

Bacon-Top Meatloaf

Lori Simmons
Princeville, IL

*Bacon with chili and Worcestershire sauces gives this meatloaf
lots of flavor. Feel free to add more chili sauce and cheese!
Some crumbled crisp bacon may also be added to the beef mixture.*

2 lbs. ground beef
1/2 c. chili sauce
1 T. Worcestershire sauce
2 eggs, beaten

1 onion, chopped
1 c. shredded Cheddar cheese
2/3 c. soft bread crumbs
1/2 lb. bacon

Crumble beef into a bowl; add remaining ingredients except bacon.
Form into a loaf; place on a rack in an ungreased 9"x5" loaf pan.
Arrange bacon slices on top. Bake, uncovered, at 350 degrees for
70 to 80 minutes, until bacon is crisp and meatloaf is no longer pink
inside. Makes 8 to 10 servings.

To mix up a no-mess meatloaf, place all the ingredients in
a large plastic zipping bag. Seal the bag and squish it until
everything is well combined...then just toss the empty bag!

Slow-Cooker Creamed Chicken

Sandra Monroe
Preston, MD

This is the best creamed chicken our family has ever eaten...
and it takes almost no effort to make!

4 boneless, skinless chicken
  breasts
1/2 c. water
1-oz. pkg. Italian salad dressing
  mix
8-oz. pkg. cream cheese,
  softened

10-3/4 oz. can cream of
  chicken soup
4-oz. can sliced mushrooms,
  drained
cooked rice or egg noodles

Place chicken in a slow cooker sprayed with non-stick vegetable
spray. Combine water and dressing mix in a cup; spoon over chicken.
Cover and cook on low setting for 3 hours. In a bowl, blend cream
cheese, soup and mushrooms. Spoon over chicken; stir gently. Cover
and cook on low setting for one additional hour, or until chicken juices
run clear. Serve chicken and sauce over cooked rice or noodles. Makes
4 servings.

A crisp green salad goes well with creamy main dishes.
For a zippy lemon dressing, shake up 1/2 cup olive oil,
1/3 cup fresh lemon juice and one tablespoon of Dijon
mustard in a jar. Chill to blend.

Cheesy Chicken & Tots Casserole

Dana Rowan
Spokane, WA

This recipe can be put together in a jiffy, as I always have the ingredients on hand. Feel free to use your own favorite cheese.

32-oz. pkg. frozen potato puffs, divided
1 to 1-1/2 3-oz. pkgs. ready-to-use bacon pieces, divided
2 c. shredded sharp Cheddar cheese

1 lb. boneless, skinless chicken breast, diced
garlic salt and Montreal steak seasoning or salt and pepper to taste
3/4 c. milk

To a slow cooker sprayed with non-stick vegetable spray, add half of the frozen potato puffs. Sprinkle with 1/3 each of bacon pieces and cheese. Add chicken; season as desired. Top with another 1/3 each of bacon and cheese. Arrange remaining potato puffs, bacon and cheese on top. Pour milk evenly over the top. Cover and cook on low setting for 4 to 6 hours. Makes 6 to 8 servings.

Create a fall centerpiece in a snap! Hot glue ears of mini Indian corn around a terra cotta pot and set a vase of orange or yellow mums in the center.

Easy Turkey Dinner

Marlene Burns
Swisher, IA

*A slow-cooker harvest recipe that's easy and good for
the harried cook! Add some cranberry sauce and dinner is served.*

4 to 6 potatoes, peeled and cut
    into large cubes
2 c. carrots, peeled and sliced
1 onion, chopped
2 lbs. boneless, skinless turkey
    thighs

10-3/4 oz. can cream of
    mushroom soup
2/3 c. chicken broth or water
1/4 c. all-purpose flour
2 T. onion soup mix

Place vegetables in a slow cooker; top with turkey. Combine
remaining ingredients in a bowl; spoon over turkey. Cover and cook
on high setting for 30 minutes. Turn setting to low. Cook for an
additional 7 hours, or until turkey juices run clear. Serves 4 to 6.

Bountiful Harvest Relish

Arlene Smulski
Lyons, IL

*I have made this tasty relish often for fall celebrations. It gives warm
rolls a real boost...great as a side dish for poultry too. My family &
friends always scrape out their jars!*

12-oz. pkg. fresh cranberries
2 firm pears, peeled and cored
1/2 lemon, seeds removed

1 T. honey
1/2 c. sugar
1/8 t. salt

Finely chop cranberries, pears and lemon in a food processor or with
a sharp knife. Combine with honey, sugar and salt; mix well. Spoon
into small jars; cover tightly. Keep refrigerated up to 2 weeks. Makes
2 half-pint jars.

For an easy harvest centerpiece, pile Jack-be-Little and
Baby Boo pumpkins on your favorite cake stand.

Crazy-Day Turkey Breast

Ali Seay
Baltimore, MD

This is a great recipe tossed together out of desperation that turned into a family favorite. Slow-cooker juices may be thickened for an easy turkey gravy, if you like.

4-lb. boneless turkey breast
2 to 4 T. butter, sliced

Cajun seasoning or seasoned
   salt to taste

Place turkey breast in a slow cooker, skin-side up. Dot with butter; rub in or spread as evenly as possible over top of breast. Sprinkle generously with desired seasoning. Cover and cook on low setting for 6 to 8 hours, until no longer pink in the center. Remove to a serving platter; let stand for 10 minutes before slicing. Serves 6 to 8.

Skillet Candied Sweet Potatoes

Krista Marshall
Fort Wayne, IN

We love sweet potatoes, and I'm always looking for new ways to prepare them. This recipe came about when I was short on time and craving something sweet. It's a winner!

5 T. butter, divided
3 to 4 sweet potatoes, peeled
   and cut into 1-inch cubes

salt and pepper to taste
1/4 c. brown sugar, packed
1-1/2 t. cinnamon

In a Dutch oven, melt 3 tablespoons butter over medium-high heat. Add sweet potatoes. Sauté for 10 to 15 minutes, until golden on all sides, stirring often. Season with salt and pepper. Push potatoes to outer edges of skillet. Melt remaining butter; sprinkle with brown sugar and stir to coat potatoes. Reduce heat to low. Cook for 15 to 20 minutes, until potatoes are fork-tender and glazed. Serves 4.

Shredded Beef over Rice

Joan Mikiten
Shavano Park, TX

*My son and his friends love this delicious slow-cooked beef
as a second dinner after Friday night football games.*

4-lb. boneless beef top
  chuck roast
1-oz. pkg. fajita seasoning
  mix, divided
2 T. canola oil
14-1/2 oz. can diced tomatoes

14-1/2 oz. can Mexican-
  seasoned stewed tomatoes
salt and pepper to taste
3/4 c. water
4 c. cooked rice
2 T. fresh parsley, chopped

Rub both sides of roast with 2 to 3 teaspoons of seasoning mix. Heat oil in a large Dutch oven over medium-high heat. Add roast and brown on all sides, about 5 minutes. Transfer roast to a slow cooker. Add tomatoes with juice, water and remaining seasoning mix. Cover and cook on high setting for 3 to 4 hours. Reduce to low setting; cook for 2 to 3 hours, until roast is very tender. Remove roast and shred, using 2 forks. Pour tomato gravy from slow cooker into a large glass bowl; skim off any fat. Add salt and pepper as needed. Stir shredded beef into tomato gravy. Combine cooked rice and parsley. Serve beef mixture over rice. Makes 8 to 12 servings.

All-day slow cooking works wonders on inexpensive,
less-tender cuts of beef. Chuck roast, round steak and
stew beef cook up juicy and delicious.

Country-Style Steak

Jewel Sharpe
Raleigh, NC

Easy-peasy in your slow cooker and so delicious. Just a few
ingredients and a side of biscuits to sop up all the gravy!

8 to 10 beef cube steaks
pepper to taste
1.35-oz. pkg onion soup mix
3/4 c. water

2 10-3/4 oz. cans cream of
   mushroom soup
warm biscuits or mashed
   potatoes

Season steaks with pepper; layer in a slow cooker. Stir together soup mix and water in a cup; spread evenly over steaks. Spoon soup over steaks; do not stir. Cover and cook on high setting for 5 to 6 hours, or on low setting for 8 hours, until steaks are tender. Serve steaks and gravy from slow cooker with biscuits or potatoes. Makes 8 to 10 servings.

My grandparents lived on a small farm in northern Indiana. I remember that as a small girl I would follow my grandpa all around. Mom said whenever he picked up his foot, my foot was right behind his...occasionally he stopped and I would run into him. He loved it! Of 21 grandkids, I was the only one who did this. We never talked, I was too shy and he was happy just to have me there. I remember all the pigs and cows we fed, the vegetables that we planted and then picked. Another favorite memory is of making applesauce with Mom's entire family of six brothers and sisters. All my aunts and uncles along with the grandkids would come over and we would pick apples. My grandma, mom and aunts would cut up the apples and put them in a huge copper kettle over a wood fire. The applesauce cooked for hours, even all day. I always had so much fun with my family.

–Pam Kollar, South Bend, IN

Autumn Pork Chops

Bianca Erickson
Hidden Valley Lake, CA

This slow-cooker recipe has the perfect flavors for fall!
So tender and juicy, it's sure to be a hit at the dinner table.

4 pork chops, divided
1 acorn squash, cut into 4 to
   6 slices and seeds removed
5 carrots, peeled and chopped
3/4 c. brown sugar, packed
2 T. butter, melted

3/4 t. browning and seasoning
   sauce
3/4 t. salt
1/2 t. orange zest
1 t. orange juice

Arrange 2 pork chops in a slow cooker. Place squash and carrots on top of chops; add remaining chops. In a small bowl, stir together remaining ingredients; spoon over chops. Cover and cook on low setting for 4 to 6 hours, until chops are no longer pink in the center. Makes 4 servings.

Autumn is a good time to check your spice rack for freshness.
Crush a pinch of each spice...if it has a fresh, zingy scent,
it's still good. Toss out any old-smelling spices and
stock up on ones you've used up during the year.

Slow-Cooked Pork Chop Dinner
Helen Adams
Enchanted Oaks, TX

This is a wonderful dish and makes a very thick rich gravy. I used to make it for my children when they were in school. Years later, it has been handed on and they are making for their own families. Be prepared for the heavenly smell while it is cooking!

4 to 6 thick-cut pork chops
2 t. dried thyme, divided
4 Yukon gold potatoes, sliced
1 yellow onion, sliced
12 mushrooms, halved

salt and pepper to taste
6 slices American cheese
10-3/4 oz. can cream of
   mushroom soup
12-oz. can evaporated milk

Season pork chops with one teaspoon thyme. Season vegetables with remaining thyme, salt and pepper; set aside. In a dry skillet over medium-high heat, brown chops on both sides. In a slow cooker, layer chops, potatoes, onion and mushrooms. Arrange cheese slices on top. Mix together soup and milk in a bowl; spoon over cheese. Cover and cook on high setting for 4 hours, or on low setting for 6 hours. Makes 4 to 6 servings.

To get rid of an onion smell after slicing, simply hold
your hands under cold running water along with
a stainless steel spoon or other utensil.

Coal Miners' Stew

Christine Jaworski
Riverside, RI

This simple dish was one of my father's favorites. After he retired,
he would make it himself and have it waiting in the slow cooker
for my mother when she got home.

4 potatoes, peeled and sliced
16-oz. pkg. Kielbasa sausage,
  sliced
2 14-1/2 oz. cans green beans,
  drained
1 onion, chopped

2 cloves garlic, minced
2 10-3/4 oz. cans cream of
  mushroom soup
1 to 2 c. shredded Cheddar
  cheese

Layer all ingredients in a slow cooker in the order given. Cover and
cook on low setting for 6 to 8 hours. Makes 6 servings.

Baking Powder Biscuits

Jenna Hord
Mount Vernon, OH

My grandma and her mother used to make these tender biscuits...
perfect for a hearty breakfast or supper!

2 c. all-purpose flour
1 T. baking powder
1 t. salt

1/4 c. shortening
3/4 c. milk

In a bowl, sift together flour, baking powder and salt. Cut in
shortening with 2 knives or a fork until mixture is as coarse as
cornmeal. Add milk; stir just enough to make a soft dough. Turn out
dough onto a lightly floured surface; knead for about 30 seconds. Roll
out dough 1/2-inch thick. Cut out biscuits with a floured 2-inch round
cutter. Place biscuits one inch apart on ungreased baking sheets. Bake
at 450 degrees for 12 to 15 minutes, until golden. Makes 15 to 18.

All seasons sweet, but autumn best of all.

–Elinor Wylie

❁ SPEEDY ❁
Suppers & Sides

All-in-One Bean Dinner

Kendra Randol
Pella, IA

Old-fashioned flavor made easy by a slow cooker! Serve with a side of cornbread for the ultimate comfort food.

1 smoked ham shank
2 c. cabbage, chopped
1 c. onion, chopped
2 to 3 potatoes, peeled and
   cut into 1-inch cubes

2 carrots, peeled and sliced
   1/2-inch thick
24-oz. jar Great Northern beans
1 c. water
pepper to taste

Place ham shank in a slow cooker. Layer chopped vegetables around ham shank; pour in beans with their liquid. Add water; season with pepper. Cover and cook on low setting for 8 to 10 hours. Remove ham shank; slice meat from the bone and stir into mixture in slow cooker. Serves 4 to 6.

Easy Corn Fritters

Eleanor Dionne
Beverly, MA

These fritters are crisp on the outside and soufflé-like on the inside.

2 eggs, separated
6 ears corn, kernels cut off,
   or 3 c. frozen corn
3 T. milk

2 T. all-purpose flour
1/2 t. salt
Garnish: maple syrup, butter

In a bowl, beat egg yolks until light yellow. Add corn, milk, flour and salt; blend well. In a separate bowl, beat egg whites with an electric mixer on medium speed until soft peaks form. Fold into corn mixture. Drop batter by rounded tablespoonfuls onto a hot greased griddle. Cook until golden on both sides. Serve hot with maple syrup and butter. Serves 4.

165

Harvest Chicken & Apples

Kathleen Bell
Clovis, CA

An easy and delicious slow-cooker recipe to make after
a visit to your favorite apple orchard.

2 c. onions, thickly sliced
2 to 3 apples, peeled, cored and
   thickly sliced
2 lbs. bone-in chicken pieces
2 T. fresh rosemary, chopped
1/2 t. salt

1/4 t. pepper
10-3/4 oz. can cream of celery
   soup
1 c. chicken broth
cooked rice

Arrange onions and apple slices in a slow cooker. Season chicken pieces with rosemary, salt and pepper; arrange over apples. Whisk together soup and broth in a bowl; spoon over chicken. Cover and cook on low setting for 6 to 8 hours, or on high setting for 3 to 4 hours. Serve over cooked rice. Serves 4 to 6.

Come, ye thankful people, come,
Raise the song of harvest home!
–Henry Alford

❊ SPEEDY ❊
Suppers & Sides

Slow-Cooker Scalloped Potatoes

Jessica Shrout
Flintstone, MD

A rich and cheesy adaptation of a favorite baked recipe.
It's wonderful for potlucks and get-togethers. Sometimes I'll add
a few unpeeled, sliced redskin potatoes for a bit of color.

4 lbs. potatoes, peeled, sliced
  and divided
2 T. butter, sliced
1 onion, diced and divided
16-oz. pkg. thick-cut bacon,
  diced and divided
3 c. shredded Cheddar cheese,
  divided

8-oz. pkg. cream cheese, cubed
  and divided
2 10-3/4 oz. cans cream of
  chicken soup
dried parsley, salt and pepper
  to taste

Arrange half of the potato slices in a large slow cooker; dot with butter. Top with half each of the onion, uncooked bacon and cheeses; repeat layers. Top with soup and seasonings. Cover and cook on low setting for 8 to 10 hours, until bubbly and potatoes are tender. Makes 8 to 10 servings.

A frozen turkey needs to begin thawing about 4 days before it's roasted. Just tuck it in the back of the refrigerator where it's coolest. Oops...you forgot? Place the turkey in a large picnic cooler and cover with cold water, changing the water once an hour. A 12 to 14-pound bird will thaw in about 8 hours.

Baked Butternut Squash

Mary King
Ashville, AL

I can still smell the cinnamon baking when my mother and grandmother used to make this recipe. I have served this yummy squash to my husband and he loves it too. One medium butternut squash serves two, so it's simple to double this recipe.

1 butternut squash, halved and
    seeds removed
2 T. butter

2 to 4 T. brown sugar, packed
2 t. cinnamon

Place squash halves cut-side down on an ungreased baking sheet. Bake at 350 degrees for 15 to 20 minutes. Turn squash halves over; top each half with one tablespoon butter, one to 2 tablespoons brown sugar and one teaspoon cinnamon. Bake at 350 degrees for an additional 30 to 40 minutes, until fork-tender. Makes 2 servings.

On clear, crisp autumn days, freshen household quilts and blankets for winter. Simply shake them out and spread over a porch rail or fence. Sunshine and fresh air will quickly chase away any mustiness that they've picked up in storage.

Fried Autumn Apples

Hollie Moots
Marysville, OH

We have been taking family trips to the apple orchard for many years. This quick dish is a favorite year 'round, but is extra special made with apples we picked together!

6 apples, peeled, cored
   and sliced
1 t. lemon juice
1/4 c. butter, sliced

1/4 c. brown sugar, packed
1 t. cinnamon
1/4 t. nutmeg
1/4 t. salt

In a bowl, toss apples with lemon juice; set aside. Melt butter in a skillet over medium-low heat. Add apples; top with brown sugar, spices and salt. Sauté, uncovered, for about 15 minutes, until apples are tender, stirring occasionally. Makes 6 servings.

Sprinkle the inside of your Jack-o'-Lantern with some pumpkin pie spice. It will smell delicious when the candle is lit!

169

Farm-Style Green Beans

Cindy Neel
Gooseberry Patch

Good old-fashioned simmered green beans are delicious! Long cooking over low heat is the secret to the farm-style taste. The beans simmer on the stove while you're doing other things...it's not a recipe to rush! In the summertime, follow these directions using about four pounds of fresh green beans.

4 slices center-cut bacon
4 14-1/2 oz. cans whole green
   beans, partially drained

1/4 c. butter, sliced
1/8 t. salt

In a large saucepan over medium heat, cook bacon until crisp. Reserve bacon and drippings in skillet. Add green beans along with enough of their liquid to cover the beans. Add butter and salt. Reduce heat to low. Cover and simmer over low heat for 2 to 3 hours. Stir occasionally, checking to make sure beans are still covered with liquid. Makes 8 to 10 servings.

Let the kids help out with the Thanksgiving feast.
Something as simple as setting the table and folding napkins
means time spent together, making memories.

❁ SPEEDY ❁
Suppers & Sides

Spinach & Cheese Puff

Regina Wickline
Pebble Beach, CA

Spinach is dressed up for the holiday table in this creamy,
cheesy dish. It takes just a few minutes to put together.

3 10-oz. pkgs. frozen chopped
    spinach, thawed and
    squeezed dry
1-1/2 c. half-and-half
3 eggs, beaten

1-1/2 c. shredded Swiss cheese,
    divided
2 t. salt
1/8 t. pepper
1/4 t. nutmeg

In a large bowl, combine spinach, half-and-half, eggs, one cup cheese
and seasonings; stir to combine. Spread mixture evenly in a lightly
greased shallow 2-quart casserole dish. Top with remaining cheese.
Bake, uncovered, at 350 degrees for 30 to 35 minutes, until set and
golden on top. Makes 8 servings.

Younger guests will feel so grown-up when served bubbly
sparkling cider or ginger ale in long-stemmed plastic glasses.
Decorate with curling ribbon just for fun.

171

Vickie's Country Sage Dressing

Vickie

*My own tried & true recipe! Toss the bread mixture well
to make sure all the bread is coated in buttery goodness.*

1-lb. loaf country white
    sandwich bread, torn
1 c. butter, sliced
1 c. onion, chopped
1 c. celery, chopped

8 to 10 fresh sage leaves,
    chopped
5 T. fresh parsley, chopped
salt and pepper to taste
1-1/2 to 2 c. chicken broth

The day before, place bread pieces on a baking sheet; allow to dry
overnight. Melt butter in a skillet over medium heat. Sauté onion and
celery until softened, about 5 minutes. In a large bowl, combine
bread, onion mixture, herbs, salt and pepper. Toss gently to coat bread
well. Spoon into a greased deep 13"x9" baking pan or a roaster pan.
Pour 1-1/2 cups broth over the top; add remaining broth if a moister
consistency is preferred. Cover; bake at 350 degrees for 30 minutes.
Uncover during the last 10 minutes to allow the bread to crisp. Makes
8 to 10 servings.

Do you have lots of leftover turkey? It freezes well for up to
three months. Cut turkey into bite-size pieces, place in plastic
freezer bags and pop in the freezer...ready to stir into
hearty casseroles and soups whenever you are.

❀ SPEEDY ❀
Suppers & Sides

Patty's Mushroom Supreme

Jennifer Salberg
Helendale, CA

One Thanksgiving, my husband's sister Patty introduced me to this recipe. I was not a big fan of mushrooms, but this is such a wonderful combination of flavors that it's a special treat. Sadly, Patty passed away before the following Thanksgiving. It is now on the menu for every holiday dinner we prepare in our home.

2 cubes beef bouillon
1/2 c. boiling water
1 lb. whole mushrooms,
   trimmed
1/2 c. butter, divided
2 T. all-purpose flour
1/2 c. whipping cream

1/8 t. salt
1/8 t. pepper
1/2 c. dry bread crumbs or
   cracker crumbs
1/2 to 1 c. grated Parmesan
   cheese

In a cup, combine bouillon cubes and boiling water; set aside. In a large skillet over medium-high heat, sauté mushrooms in 1/4 cup butter. Transfer mixture to a greased 2-quart casserole dish; set aside. Melt remaining butter; blend with flour in a large bowl. Stir in cream, bouillon mixture, salt and pepper. Pour cream mixture over mushrooms. In a small bowl, mix crumbs and cheese; sprinkle on top. Bake, uncovered, at 350 degrees for 30 minutes, until bubbly and golden. May bake the day before, cover and refrigerate for reheating. Serves 6 to 8.

Make your own bread crumbs. Save leftover bread slices (the "heels" are fine) and freeze in a plastic bag. When you have enough, bake the slices in a 250-degree oven until dry and crumbly, then tear into sections and pulse in a food processor or blender.

Yellow Squash Casserole

Lisanne Miller
Canton, MS

A light casserole for Thanksgiving dinner that tastes wonderful!
You can use fresh or frozen yellow squash. This may be made
ahead and it's easy to double.

2 to 3 c. yellow squash,
   thinly sliced
1/2 c. mayonnaise
1/2 c. shredded Cheddar cheese
1/4 c. green pepper, minced
2 T. green onions, minced

1 egg, beaten
pepper to taste
1 sleeve round buttery crackers,
   crushed
1/4 c. butter, melted

In a large saucepan, bring one inch of water to a boil over high heat.
Add squash. Reduce heat to medium; cover and cook for 3 to
5 minutes, or until fork-tender. Drain well and let cool; transfer
squash to a large bowl. Add remaining ingredients except crackers
and butter; mix well. Spoon squash mixture into a lightly greased
2-quart casserole dish. Mix crackers with melted butter in a separate
bowl; spread on top. Bake, uncovered, at 350 degrees for 20 to
25 minutes, until golden. Serves 4 to 6.

If it's Thanksgiving now, Christmas can't be far away.
Why not double any must-have casseroles or side dishes and
freeze half for Christmas dinner...you'll be so glad you did!

Savory Baked Potatoes

Martha Stephens
Covington, LA

I'm always looking for different new ways to fix potatoes instead of the same ol' baked potatoes. So I created this...my kids love it!

5 to 6 russet potatoes, very
    thinly sliced and divided
1/4 c. extra-virgin olive oil,
    divided
2 t. garlic powder

2 t. seasoned salt
1/2 t. celery salt
2 t. salt
2 t. pepper
Garnish: dried parsley

Arrange half of the potato slices in a greased 13"x9" glass baking pan. Drizzle with half of the oil. Combine all seasonings except garnish; sprinkle half of mixture over potatoes. Repeat layers; sprinkle parsley on top. Cover with aluminum foil. Bake at 375 degrees for 35 to 45 minutes, until potatoes are tender. Serves 6.

A day or two before Turkey Day, set out all the serving platters, baskets and dishes and label them..."Judy's Cranberry Sauce," "Grandma's Muffins" and so on. When the time arrives, you'll be able to get dinner on the table in a jiffy.

Festive Broccoli Salad

Crystal Shook
Catawba, NC

This crunchy salad goes well with just about any meal. It's perfect for school potlucks, tailgating parties and even Thanksgiving.

3 bunches broccoli, cut into
  bite-size flowerets
1/2 c. sweetened dried
  cranberries
1/3 c. toasted almonds
  or pecans

1 onion, chopped
1 c. mayonnaise
1/3 c. sugar
2 T. cider vinegar
6 slices bacon, crisply cooked
  and crumbled

In a large bowl, toss together broccoli, cranberries, nuts and onion; set aside. In a separate bowl, mix mayonnaise, sugar and vinegar; spoon over broccoli mixture and toss to mix. Top with bacon. Cover and refrigerate for 2 to 4 hours. Serves 8 to 10.

Lynn's Nutty Slaw

Lynn Foley
Branson, MO

This slaw may sound a little unusual, but it's delicious, oh-so easy to make and keeps really well in the fridge.

16-oz. pkg. coleslaw mix
1/3 c. salted cocktail peanuts
1/3 c. raisins

1/2 c. mayonnaise
1 T. red wine vinegar
1 t. sugar

Combine slaw mix, peanuts and raisins in a large bowl; set aside. In a separate small bowl, combine mayonnaise, vinegar and sugar; stir until well blended. Fold mayonnaise mixture into slaw and combine well. Cover and refrigerate at least one hour before serving. Makes 6 to 8 servings.

Apple Orchard Salad

Lynn Williams
Muncie, IN

*I used to love my mom's Waldorf salad, but with a sweet dressing
and tiny marshmallows, it needed a bit of updating.
This version is fruity and refreshing.*

2 apples, peeled, cored
   and diced
1/2 c. golden raisins or
   sweetened dried cranberries

2 stalks celery, sliced
1/2 c. chopped walnuts
1/4 c. mayonnaise
2 T. orange juice

Combine all ingredients in a serving bowl; toss to mix well. Cover and
chill until serving time. Makes 6 to 8 servings.

When I was in first grade, at Thanksgiving we sang, "Over the
river and through the woods, to Grandmother's house we go."
I thought the song was written about my grandmother because
we really did have to cross a river and go through the woods to
get to her home! We traveled in a car rather than a sleigh, but
no matter...it seemed to me that most details were correct!
When we got to her old farmhouse, we would see a table that
was groaning from all the food placed on it. There was always a
big roast goose, many vegetable casseroles, fluffy mashed
potatoes, gravy and other delights. Cakes, pies and puddings
were brought in after we had eaten the main course. Everyone
talked, laughed and just enjoyed being together. What fond
memories I have of those times

–Dee Lakes, Mansfield, OH

Creamy Cranberry Salad

Lynda Robson
Boston, MA

An easy make-ahead for your Thanksgiving buffet.

14-oz. can whole-berry
  cranberry sauce
1 c. boiling water
3-oz. pkg. strawberry gelatin
  mix

1 T. lemon juice
1/2 c. mayonnaise
1 apple, peeled, cored and diced
1/4 c. chopped pecans

Spoon cranberry sauce into a small saucepan over low heat; cook
until melted. Strain, reserving cranberry juice; set cranberries aside.
In a bowl, combine reserved cranberry juice, boiling water and dry
gelatin mix; stir until dissolved. Stir in lemon juice. Cover and
refrigerate until gelatin begins to set. Add mayonnaise; beat with an
electric mixer on low speed until fluffy. Fold in reserved cranberries,
apple and pecans; pour into a 4-cup mold. Cover and refrigerate until
set. Turn out of mold onto a serving plate. Makes 6 servings.

Picture-perfect portions of a favorite gelatin salad are
handy for buffets or potlucks. Spoon the gelatin mixture
into paper muffin liners and set in a baking pan. Chill until
firm, then peel off liners.

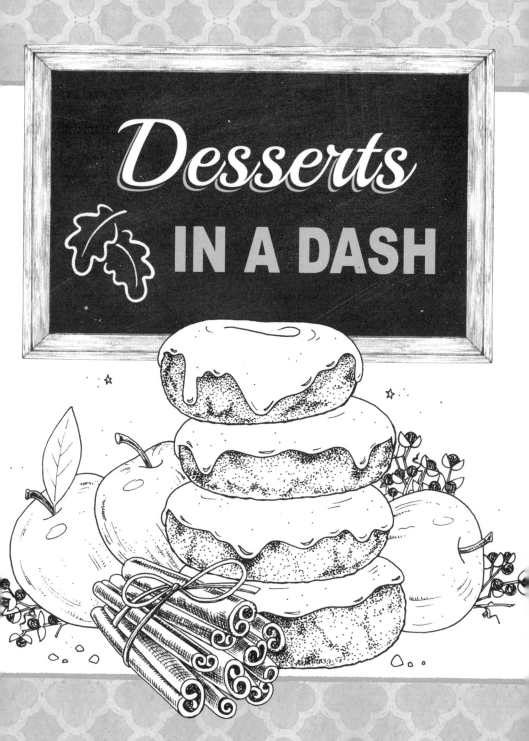

Desserts

IN A DASH

Nanny's Peanut Butter Goblins
Beverly Mahorney
Cynthiana, KY

Every year on Halloween my family hosts an open house. My mom always made these simple but scrumptious cookies for it. We lost her in 2005, but when I make her cookies, I feel like she's still with us.

1-1/2 c. all-purpose flour
1/2 t. baking soda
1/2 t. salt
1/2 c. butter, softened
1 c. crunchy peanut butter

1/2 c. brown sugar, packed
1 c. sugar, divided
1 egg, beaten
1 t. vanilla extract

In a bowl, mix together flour, baking soda and salt; set aside. In a separate large bowl, combine butter, peanut butter, brown sugar and 1/2 cup sugar. Beat with an electric mixer on medium speed until blended; stir in egg and vanilla. Add flour mixture; stir until a stiff dough forms. Roll dough into balls by tablespoonfuls. Roll balls in remaining sugar; place 2 inches apart on greased baking sheets. With a fork dipped in sugar, flatten balls in a criss-cross pattern. Bake at 375 degrees for 10 to 12 minutes, until golden. Makes 3 dozen.

Parchment paper is a baker's best friend! Place it on a baking sheet to keep cookies from spreading and sticking. Clean-up is a breeze too. Generally, the paper can be reused at least once... when it starts to darken, toss it.

🎃 *Desserts* 🎃
IN A DASH

Speedy Little Devils

Sherry Cecil
South Point, OH

When I was a child. this was my "special treat" that Mom made for me. Little did I know back then how just a few simple ingredients could make such a delicious rich dessert. Now that I have my own family, this has become one of my kids' favorite desserts and always takes me back to fond memories from my childhood!

18-1/4 oz. pkg. devil's food
   cake mix
1/2 c. butter, melted

1/2 c. creamy peanut butter
7-oz. jar marshmallow creme

In a large bowl, combine dry cake mix with melted butter; mix well. Reserve 1-1/2 cups of cake mixture for topping. Press remaining cake mixture into the bottom of an ungreased 13"x9" baking pan. In a separate bowl, blend peanut butter and marshmallow creme; gently spread over cake mixture. Sprinkle remaining cake mixture over top. Bake at 350 degrees for 20 minutes. Cool; cut into squares. Makes one dozen.

When I think of harvest time, it brings such wonderful memories of my mother. She was a great cook and our house was filled with the best smells. Coming in the back door after a crisp fall walk home from school, I was always greeted by my mother in her ruffled apron and the smell of homemade breads, cakes and cookies, yum! But my best 'smell' memory was her bread pudding. The egg custard mixed with bread, plump raisins and the cinnamon with just a dash of nutmeg added to it. Oh my goodness, my mouth just waters when I think of it.

–Ann Viviano, St. John, IN

Fruity Sugar Cookies

Rita Jefferis
Anthony, KS

A co-worker gave me this great recipe more than 20 years ago. These bright-colored cookies are beautiful for any special occasion. I've used it for many school parties. It's an easy dough for beginning bakers to handle. Finish it simply by sprinkling the tops with a little sugar before baking, if you wish to skip the decorator icing.

3 c. all-purpose flour
1 t. baking powder
1 t. salt
1 c. sugar
3-oz. pkg. favorite-flavor
   gelatin mix

3/4 c. shortening
2 eggs, beaten
Optional: additional sugar
   for sprinkling, decorator
   frosting

In a bowl, mix together flour, baking powder and salt; set aside. In a separate bowl, combine sugar and dry gelatin mix; stir well. Add shortening and eggs; mix until smooth. Add flour mixture; stir well until a soft dough forms. Roll out dough on a lightly floured surface. Cut out desired shapes with cookie cutters. Arrange cookies on baking sheets lightly sprayed with non-stick vegetable spray. Sprinkle with sugar, if desired. Bake at 375 degrees for 6 to 8 minutes. Cool cookies on wire racks; decorate with frosting, if desired. Makes 4 dozen.

When rolling out cookie dough, sprinkle powdered sugar
on the work surface. So much tastier than using flour
and it works just as well!

Desserts
IN A DASH

Judy's Brownie Cookies

Judy Borecky
Escondido, CA

My husband loves these cookies...and who wouldn't,
with chocolate chips, cranberries and crunchy oats?

20-oz. pkg. brownie mix
1-1/2 c. quick-cooking oats,
   uncooked
1/2 c. oil
2 eggs, beaten

1/2 c. semi-sweet chocolate
   chips
1/2 c. sweetened dried
   cranberries
Optional: pecan halves

In a large bowl, combine dry brownie mix, oats, oil and eggs; mix
well. Stir in chocolate chips and cranberries. Drop dough by rounded
teaspoons onto ungreased baking sheets. If desired, press 3 to
4 pecan halves onto the top of each cookie. Bake, one sheet at a time,
at 350 degrees for 15 to 17 minutes. Let cookies cool for 2 minutes;
remove to wire racks and cool completely. Makes 2 dozen.

Nut Macaroons

Rebecca Etling
Blairsville, PA

One of my favorite quick & easy cookie recipes.

2/3 c. sweetened
   condensed milk
1 c. sweetened flaked coconut

1 c. chopped nuts
1 t. vanilla extract
3/4 t. almond extract

In a bowl, mix all ingredients in the order given. Drop by teaspoonfuls
onto well greased baking sheets. Bake at 350 degrees for 10 to
12 minutes, until dry around the edges. Makes 2 dozen.

When baking two sheets of cookies
at once, remember to reverse the
top and bottom sheets halfway
through the baking time to
ensure they bake evenly.

Butterscotch Cherry Cookies

Renae Scheiderer
Beallsville, OH

A friend shared the recipe for these cookies...they are delicious!

2 c. all-purpose flour
1 t. baking soda
1 t. salt
1 c. butter, softened
1 c. sugar

1 t. vanilla extract
6-oz. pkg. butterscotch chips
1/2 c. chopped pecans
1/2 c. maraschino cherries,
    well drained and chopped

Combine flour, baking soda and salt in a bowl; mix well and set aside.
In a separate large bowl, combine butter and sugar; beat until creamy.
Blend in vanilla. Add flour mixture and stir well. Fold in butterscotch
chips, pecans and cherries. Drop dough by rounded teaspoonfuls onto
ungreased baking sheets. Bake at 375 degrees for 10 to 12 minutes,
until golden. Makes 7 dozen.

Little ones love to help out in the kitchen, so tuck
a set of measuring spoons, oven mitt and mini rolling pin
in the pocket of a child-size apron...everything
a little helper needs.

Lemon Pecan Dainties

Cassie Hooker
La Porte, TX

You'll love these tender, lemony cookies...perfect with a cup of tea.

2 c. all-purpose flour
1 t. baking powder
1/2 t. salt
3/4 c. shortening
1 c. sugar

1 egg, beaten
1 T. lemon zest
1 T. lemon juice
1 c. pecans, finely chopped

In a bowl, mix together flour, baking powder and salt; set aside. In a separate large bowl, combine shortening and sugar; blend very well. Add egg, lemon zest and lemon juice; beat well. Add flour mixture and mix well; stir in pecans. Shape dough into rolls, 2 inches thick. Wrap in plastic wrap; chill thoroughly. Slice very thinly, about 1/4-inch thick. Place on greased baking sheets. Bake at 350 degrees for 12 to 15 minutes. Cool slightly before removing from baking sheets. Makes 4 dozen.

Such a thoughtful gift for a busy mom! Wrap up a roll of your best cookie dough along with fun decorations...colorful sprinkles, candy-coated chocolates and of course a cookie cutter or two. She'll love it!

Delicious Cranberry Bars

Susan Wilson
Johnson City, TN

My husband loves these bar cookies any time of the year. They are especially good with a cup of hot coffee.

2 c. all-purpose flour
2 c. long-cooking oats, uncooked
1 c. sugar

1 t. baking powder
1 c. butter, melted
2 14-oz. cans whole-berry cranberry sauce

In a large bowl, combine all ingredients except cranberry sauce; mix until large crumbs form. Reserve 1-1/2 cups of crumb mixture for topping. Press remaining crumb mixture into the bottom of a greased and floured 13"x9" baking pan. Spread cranberry sauce over top. Sprinkle with reserved crumb mixture; pat gently. Bake at 350 degrees for 25 minutes. Cool and cut into bars. Store in refrigerator. Makes 1-1/2 dozen.

Serve up a Bucket o' Bones at your next Halloween party! Press a mini marshmallow into each end of a pretzel stick and dip in melted white chocolate.

Beth's Toffee Bars

Beth Richter
Canby, MN

This recipe gets taken everywhere! From the first time I made these bars, they have always been in high demand. At family gatherings, they often disappear as fast as they hit the table...they're that good!

18-1/2 oz. pkg. yellow cake mix
1 egg, beaten
1/3 c. butter, melted and slightly
   cooled

6-oz. pkg. toffee bits
14-oz. can sweetened
   condensed milk

In a large bowl, stir together dry cake mix, egg and butter. Gently pat into a 13"x9" baking pan. Sprinkle with toffee bits; spread condensed milk over the top. Bake at 350 degrees for about 25 minutes. Cool; cut into squares. Makes about 16 bars.

A vintage black lunchbox makes a clever Halloween candy holder...just fill with tasty treats for little goblins to choose from.

Delectable Peanut Butter Squares

Lyn Peters
Olive Hill, KY

When I was in grade school, our cafeteria had these melty peanut butter
& chocolate squares. After searching for years for the recipe, I decided
that it was time to tackle the task myself. After much trial & error,
I have come close to the ones I remember as a child.

1/2 c. butter
1/2 c. brown sugar, packed
2 c. creamy or crunchy peanut
   butter

1 t. vanilla extract
2-1/2 c. powdered sugar
6-oz. pkg. semi-sweet chocolate
   chips

Melt butter in a large saucepan over low heat, stirring to prevent
burning. Add brown sugar; stir until completely dissolved. Add peanut
butter and vanilla; mix thoroughly. Add powdered sugar; stir well.
Press mixture into a 13"x9" baking pan sprayed with non-stick
vegetable spray; let cool. Melt chocolate chips in a double boiler over
low heat; spread evenly over peanut butter layer. Let cool completely;
cut into squares. Makes one to 2 dozen.

Slice bar cookies into one-inch squares and set them in
frilly paper candy cups. Guests will love sampling "just a bite"
of several different treats.

Desserts

IN A DASH

Marbled Chocolate Bars

Darlene Hartzler
Marshallville, OH

This super-easy recipe is a lunchbox favorite for my kids.

18-1/4 oz. pkg. German
   chocolate cake mix
8-oz. pkg. cream cheese,
   softened

1/2 c. sugar
3/4 c. milk chocolate chips,
   divided

Prepare cake batter according to package directions. Spread in a greased 15"x10" jelly-roll pan; set aside. In a separate bowl, beat together cream cheese and sugar; stir in 1/4 cup chocolate chips. Drop mixture by tablespoonfuls over batter; cut through batter with a knife to swirl. Sprinkle with remaining chocolate chips. Bake at 350 degrees for 25 to 30 minutes, until a toothpick inserted in the center comes out clean. Cool in pan on a wire rack. Cut into bars. Makes 3 dozen.

Warm up dinner with friends by hosting a casual fireside supper. Toast sandwiches in pie irons and make s'mores for dessert...so cozy!

Mom's Pumpkin Brownies

Linda Renderer
Ocala, FL

Mom always made these terrific brownies on Halloween
before we went out trick-or-treating.

4 eggs, room temperature
2 c. sugar
1 c. butter, melted and slightly
   cooled
1 c. canned pumpkin
1 t. vanilla extract

1-1/2 c. all-purpose flour
1-1/2 t. pumpkin pie spice
1/2 t. cinnamon
Garnish: vanilla or cream cheese
   frosting

In a large bowl, beat eggs well with an electric mixer on medium
speed. Beat in sugar, butter, pumpkin and vanilla on medium speed.
Add flour and spices; beat on low speed. Spread batter in a lightly
greased 9"x9" baking pan. Bake at 350 degrees for 40 minutes. Cool;
frost as desired and cut into squares. Makes 8 to 10.

Save the sprinkles! Before adding candy sprinkles to cookies,
cover the table with a length of wax paper. Return any excess
sprinkles to their jars by simply folding the paper in half, gently
shaking sprinkles to one side and sliding them into the jar.

7-Layer Brownie Bars

Becky Holsinger
Belpre, OH

My husband came home from work one day, talking about some delicious brownies that his co-worker had brought to work. I told him to get me the recipe and he was right...these are wonderful!

1/2 c. butter, melted
18-oz. pkg. double chocolate
    brownie mix
1 c. sweetened flaked coconut
1 c. butterscotch chips

1 c. semi-sweet chocolate chips
1 c. chopped pecans
14-oz. can sweetened
    condensed milk

Spread melted butter in the bottom of a 13"x9" baking pan; sprinkle dry brownie mix over butter. Top with coconut, butterscotch chips, chocolate chips and pecans. Drizzle with condensed milk. Bake at 350 degrees for 30 to 35 minutes, until edges are bubbly. Cool completely before cutting into bars. Makes one dozen.

Just for fun, slip a little note of encouragement
into your child's lunchbox each week.

Halloween Candy Pie

Elizabeth Cassinos
Paradise Valley, NV

I used to make this simple treat all the time for my girls when they were little. Their little faces really lit up when I served to them in a real pizza box!

12-oz. pkg. semi-sweet
  chocolate chips

1 c. dry-roasted peanuts
1 c. candy corn

Line an 8" or 9" round cake pan with parchment paper or wax paper; set aside. In a saucepan, melt chocolate chips over low heat; stir in peanuts. Pour into cake pan. Decorate with candy corn as desired. Cover and chill until firm. Turn "pizza" out of pan; peel off paper. Slice into wedges. Makes 8 servings.

Ask your neighborhood pizza parlor for a new pizza box
to put your Halloween Candy Pie in. Decorate the lid
with colorful craft paper cut-outs and stickers...don't forget
to tie on a pizza cutter!

❂ *Desserts* ❂
IN A DASH

Taffy Apple Pizza

Lori Simmons
Princeville, IL

A fun fall dessert that everyone is sure to like.

16-1/2 oz. pkg. refrigerated
    sugar cookie dough
8-oz. pkg. cream cheese,
    softened
3/4 c. brown sugar, packed

2 t. vanilla extract
4 to 6 apples, cored and sliced
Garnish: caramel ice cream
    topping
Optional: chopped peanuts

Press cookie dough into an ungreased pizza pan. Bake at 350 degrees for 10 to 12 minutes, until golden; let cool. In a bowl, blend cream cheese, brown sugar and vanilla; spread over cooled crust. Arrange apple slices on top; drizzle caramel topping over the apples. If desired, sprinkle with peanuts. Cover and chill; cut into wedges. Makes 8 to 10 servings.

Every year when fall came with apple season, we loaded the bushel baskets into our 1946 Oldsmobile, packed bologna sandwiches and Mason jars of water and headed to a neighboring orchard to pick apples. My daddy always insisted only on Jonathan apples that were almost too ripe. He cooked his apple butter in a cast-iron Dutch oven instead of a slow cooker as I do now. Daddy said his Indian grandmother would cook it over an open fire, starting before daylight and finishing up around midnight. He also taught me how to make "cathead" biscuits which we would cover with homemade Guernsey butter and the apple butter. It was delicious on just about anything. I just loved eating it out of the jar...unless I got caught!

–Cheryl Bone, Millington, TN

Sopapilla Cheesecake

Dorothy Keichler
Friendswood, TX

This recipe is the answer when you need a big tasty dessert, fast!
Mix & match your choice of fruit fillings...apple, strawberry, cherry,
blackberry, raspberry and blueberry are all wonderful.

2 8-oz. tubes crescent rolls,
   divided
3 8-oz. pkgs. cream cheese,
   softened
1-1/2 c. plus 1 T. sugar, divided

1-1/2 t. vanilla extract
2 21-oz. cans fruit pie filling,
   divided
1/2 c. butter, melted
2 T. cinnamon

Spray a 13"x9" glass baking pan with non-stick vegetable spray.
Unroll one can of crescent rolls in the bottom of pan; set aside.
Combine cream cheese, 1-1/2 cups sugar and vanilla in a large bowl.
Beat with an electric mixer on medium speed until soft and fluffy.
Spread half of cream cheese mixture over rolls. Spread one can of pie
filling on half of the cream cheese mixture, to one side, and the
remaining can on the other half. Spread remaining cream cheese
mixture over pie filling; lay remaining crescent rolls on top. Drizzle
with melted butter. Mix remaining sugar with cinnamon; sprinkle over
butter. Bake at 350 degrees for 45 minutes, or until golden. Cool
slightly; cut into squares. Makes 20 servings.

If you see a vintage cake pan with its own slide-on lid
at a tag sale, snap it up! It's indispensable for toting cakes
and bar cookies to picnics and potlucks.

Fruit Cocktail Cake

Nan Calcagno
Grosse Tete, LA

This old favorite is delicious and so easy...good for family gatherings and church dinners.

2 c. all-purpose flour
1 t. baking soda
2-1/2 c. sugar, divided
2 eggs, beaten
15-oz. can fruit cocktail in syrup

1/2 c. brown sugar, packed
1/2 c. chopped pecans
1 c. evaporated milk
1/2 c. butter, sliced

In a large bowl, stir together flour, baking soda and 1-1/2 cups sugar. Add eggs and fruit cocktail with syrup; beat well. Pour batter into a greased 13"x9" baking pan. Sprinkle with brown sugar and pecans. Bake at 325 degrees for 30 to 40 minutes; remove from oven. In a saucepan, combine remaining sugar, evaporated milk and butter over medium heat. Bring to a boil; cook and stir for several minutes, until thickened. Drizzle over warm cake; cut into squares. Makes 15 servings.

Host an outdoor movie night in your own backyard! Great fun for watching the big game on TV too. Call a local camera or rental store for a video projector...simply hook it to a DVD player and project your favorite movie on a painter's canvas dropcloth. Sure to be a hit!

Pumpkin Pudding

Joyce Stackhouse
Cadiz, OH

*This recipe is really quick to make and scrumptious...perfect for
a light dessert after a big meal. If you are watching your calories,
you can use sugar-free pudding mix and skim milk.*

2 c. milk
3.4-oz. pkg. instant vanilla
   pudding mix
1 c. canned pumpkin

1 t. vanilla extract
1 t. pumpkin pie spice
1/2 t. cinnamon
Optional: whipped cream

Combine milk and dry pudding mix in a large bowl. Beat with an
electric mixer on low speed for one to 2 minutes, until smooth. Add
pumpkin, vanilla and spices; mix well. Spoon into individual dessert
bowls; cover and chill. If desired, garnish with dollops of whipped
cream at serving time. Makes 6 to 8 servings.

Pumpkin pie is scrumptious topped with homemade
whipped cream. For the fluffiest whipped cream possible,
always make sure the bowl and beaters are chilled.

☺ *Desserts* ☺
IN A DASH

Pumpkin Gingersnap Ice Cream

Paula Purcell
Plymouth Meeting, PA

An old-fashioned shop near us used to sell this ice cream in the fall.
When the shop went out of business, I had to come up with a substitute.
We think my version is even better! A great harvest dessert, especially ·
for Thanksgiving.

14-oz. container vanilla
   ice cream, softened
15-oz. can pumpkin
1 sleeve gingersnap cookies,
   crushed

Optional: whipped cream,
   additional gingersnaps,
   candy corn

In a large bowl, combine ice cream and pumpkin; blend well by hand.
Stir in crushed cookies. Cover and freeze. If desired, garnish scoops of
ice cream with a dollop of whipped cream, a gingersnap cookie and
several pieces of candy corn. Makes 6 to 8 servings.

Looking for a new no-mess way to decorate Jack-o'-Lanterns?
Try duct tape! It comes in lots of fun colors and is super-easy
to cut into shapes...great for kids to craft with. Later, the uncut
pumpkin can even be re-purposed for pies.

Apple-Cranberry Crostada

Wendy Ball
Battle Creek, MI

A wonderful dessert using pantry ingredients! So simple, it can be baked while you're eating dinner. Some canned apple pie fillings have more filling than apples...in those cases, I add an extra apple.

21-oz. can apple pie filling
1/2 c. whole-berry cranberry
   sauce
Optional: 1 Golden Delicious
   apple, peeled, cored and
   sliced

9-inch pie crust, room
   temperature
1 egg white
1 t. water
2 to 4 T. raw or regular sugar
Garnish: ice cream

Combine pie filling and cranberry sauce in a bowl. Add sliced apple if pie filling is thin; set aside. Unroll pie crust on a sheet of wax paper. Cover with another piece of wax paper; roll out crust slightly larger. Place rolled-out pie crust onto a baking sheet that has been sprayed with non-stick spray. Spoon fruit mixture into center of pie crust, leaving a 2-inch rim. Fold edge of crust over fruit mixture, pleating crust as necessary. In a separate bowl, whisk together egg white and water. Brush crust with egg white mixture; sprinkle with sugar. Bake at 425 degrees for 15 to 18 minutes, until golden and bubbly. Leave crust uncovered to prevent softening. Serve warm, garnished as desired. Makes 6 servings.

Stir up some Grizzly Gorp for snacking and tucking into lunchboxes. Just toss together 2 cups bear-shaped graham crackers, one cup mini marshmallows, one cup peanuts and 1/2 cup seedless raisins. Yum!

🎃 *Desserts* 🎃
IN A DASH

Apple Crisp with a Twist

Natasha Crevier
London, Ontario

An old family recipe that's so simple, anyone can do it.

4 c. tart apples, cored and sliced
1/3 c. butter, softened
1 c. brown sugar, packed
3/4 c. all-purpose flour

cinnamon to taste
Optional: ice cream or whipped
   cream

Arrange apple slices in a lightly greased 8"x8" baking pan; set aside. In a bowl, mix butter, brown sugar and flour until crumbly; sprinkle over apples. Add cinnamon to taste. Bake at 350 degrees for about one hour. Serve warm, garnished as desired. Makes 6 servings.

Roly Polys

Pam Halter
Pennsville, NJ

Whenever my mom made pie, she would make these treats from the leftover crust. We kids liked them better than the pie! A few years ago, I discovered refrigerated pie crust, which is perfect for making Roly Polys. Now we can enjoy them anytime!

9-inch pie crust, room
   temperature
2 t. butter, melted

1/2 c. sugar
1 t. cinnamon

Unroll pie crust; brush with melted butter. Combine sugar and cinnamon in a cup; sprinkle over crust. Roll up crust; slice 1/2-inch thick. Place rolls cut-side up on an ungreased baking stone or a greased baking sheet. Bake at 400 degrees for 15 minutes, or until golden. Makes about 1-1/2 dozen.

An old-fashioned trick for softening unripe fruit...simply place it in a brown paper bag on the countertop. It'll ripen in no time at all.

Lemon Crunch Pound Cake

Sharon Jones
Fountain, FL

This is the best lemon pound cake I've ever made...everyone loves it!
I enjoy serving it to special morning coffee guests...my mom,
a neighbor or a group of ladies from church. I hope you love it too!

18-1/4 oz. pkg. yellow cake mix	3/4 c. water
3-oz. pkg. lemon gelatin mix	1 t. lemon extract
2/3 c. oil	1/2 t. salt
4 eggs, beaten	1/2 c. chopped pecans

In a large bowl, combine dry cake and gelatin mixes. Add remaining ingredients except pecans; beat well until smooth. Spray a Bundt® pan with non-stick vegetable spray; sprinkle with flour and shake out loose flour. Sprinkle pecans in bottom of pan; pour in batter. Bake at 325 degrees for 45 to 55 minutes, until a toothpick tests clean. Cool cake completely; turn out of pan onto a serving plate. Drizzle with Powdered Sugar Glaze shortly before serving. Makes about 12 servings.

Powdered Sugar Glaze:

2 c. powdered sugar	1/2 t. vanilla extract
3 T. milk	

Mix together powdered sugar and milk to desired thickness for drizzling; stir in vanilla.

A party without cake is really just a meeting.
–Julia Child

Poppy Seed Cake

Pamela Bennett
Whittier, CA

*I have been making this cake for parties, showers, cake walks,
fundraisers...you name it, for years! For a flavorful change,
sprinkle the greased pan with cinnamon-sugar instead of flour.*

18-1/2 oz. pkg. white or
  yellow cake mix
3.4-oz. pkg. instant lemon
  pudding mix
1 c. water

1/2 c. oil
4 eggs, beaten
1/4 c. poppy seed
1 t. almond extract

In a large bowl, mix together dry cake and pudding mixes. Add water
and oil; beat well with an electric mixer on medium speed. Beat in
eggs, one at a time. Add poppy seed and extract; beat until smooth.
Pour batter into a well greased and floured Bundt® pan. Bake at
350 degrees for about 45 minutes, until a toothpick comes out clean.
Allow cake to cool in pan for 15 minutes before removing. Drizzle
with Lemon Glaze, if desired; cake is also delicious served plain.
Makes 10 to 12 servings.

Lemon Glaze:

2 c. powdered sugar
3 T. milk

1/2 t. lemon extract

Mix together powdered sugar and milk to desired thickness for
drizzling; stir in extract.

Cover the tube in a Bundt® pan
with a small paper cup. When you
pour in the batter, it won't spill
down the center hole.

Festive Cranberry Pie

Gladys Kielar
Whitehouse, OH

For something so delicious, this takes no time at all.

2 c. fresh or frozen cranberries
1-1/2 c. sugar, divided
1/2 c. chopped walnuts
   or pecans
2 eggs

1 c. all-purpose flour
1/4 c. shortening, melted and
   slightly cooled
1/2 c. butter, melted and
   slightly cooled

Spread cranberries in a 10" deep-dish pie plate sprayed with non-stick vegetable spray. Sprinkle with 1/2 cup sugar and nuts; set aside. In a bowl, beat eggs well; gradually add remaining sugar and beat thoroughly. Add flour, shortening and butter; mix well and pour over cranberries. Bake at 325 degrees for one hour, or until bubbly and crust is golden. Makes 8 servings.

Fresh cranberries can be kept frozen up to 12 months, so if you enjoy them, stock up every autumn when they're available and pop unopened bags in the freezer. You'll be able to add their fruity tang to recipes year 'round.

Sweet Potato Pie

Lisa Barber
Tyler, TX

My mom makes this pie every year at Thanksgiving and Christmas.
It is a favorite of several family members. My son says he doesn't like
sweet potato pie, but every year he eats it and loves it because he
thinks it is pumpkin!

3 sweet potatoes, peeled and sliced	2 eggs, well beaten
1/4 c. butter, softened	1 c. evaporated milk
1/8 t. salt	1 t. cinnamon
1 c. sugar, or more to taste	1 t. vanilla extract
	9-inch pie crust

In a saucepan, cover sweet potatoes with water. Bring to a boil over
medium-high heat; boil potatoes until tender. Drain; mash potatoes
with butter, salt and sugar. Add eggs, evaporated milk, cinnamon and
vanilla; mix well. Pour into unbaked pie crust. Bake at 350 degrees
for 45 minutes. Reduce heat to 300 degrees; bake another 15 minutes,
or until pie is set. Cool before serving. Makes 8 servings.

Take time to share family stories and traditions with
your children. A cherished family recipe can be
a great conversation starter.

Pumpkin Crunch Cream Pie

Eleanor Dionne
Beverly, MA

*This is a special favorite of mine every fall...it's perfect for
Thanksgiving and so simple to make.*

3/4 c. whole milk
3.4-oz. pkg. instant vanilla
   pudding mix
1/2 c. canned pumpkin
3/4 t. pumpkin pie spice
2/3 c. semi-sweet chocolate
   chips

2/3 c. slivered almonds
12-oz. container frozen whipped
   topping, thawed and divided
9-inch graham cracker crust
Optional: chocolate curls

Pour milk into a bowl; add dry pudding mix. Beat with a whisk until
well blended; let stand for about 5 minutes. Blend in pumpkin, spice,
chocolate chips, almonds and 2 cups whipped topping. Spoon into pie
crust. Cover and chill for about 4 hours. Just before serving, garnish
with remaining whipped topping and chocolate curls, if desired.

Chocolate shavings look so delicate but are really
simple to make. Just pull a vegetable peeler across
a bar of chocolate and watch it curl!

☙ *Desserts* ☙
IN A DASH

Harvest Apple Parfait Crunch

Shirl Parsons
Cape Carteret, NC

Enjoy the flavor of fresh caramel apples in a layered dessert.
It only looks like it took a lot of effort!

8-oz. pkg. Neufchâtel cheese,
  softened
3/4 c. dark brown sugar,
  packed and divided
1 T. milk
1/2 c. granola cereal nuggets

3/4 c. dry-roasted peanuts,
  finely chopped
3 T. margarine, melted
4 red apples, cored and chopped
Garnish: whipped topping

Mix Neufchâtel cheese, 1/2 cup brown sugar and milk in a bowl until
well blended; set aside. In a separate small bowl, combine cereal,
peanuts and remaining brown sugar; stir in melted margarine until
well blended. Spoon half of the apples into 6 parfait glasses; cover
with half each of cheese mixture and cereal mixture. Add a dollop of
whipped topping. Repeat layering, ending with topping. Serve
immediately, or cover and chill. Makes 6 servings.

It's easy to make your own crumb crust. Mix 1-1/2 cups fine
crumbs, 1/4 cup sugar and 1/2 cup melted butter; press into
a pie plate. Chill for 20 minutes, or bake at 350 degrees for
10 minutes. For the crumbs, use vanilla wafers or graham
crackers, of course...try gingersnaps or pretzels too!

Ruth's Oatmeal Pie

Gloria Land
Southlake, TX

My mother used to make this recipe. It is like a pecan pie, but made with oatmeal instead of nuts...so simple. I have shared this with friends who have allergies to nuts and don't want to miss out on a Thanksgiving day favorite.

2/3 c. long-cooking oats,
    uncooked
2/3 c. sugar
2 eggs, beaten
1/3 c. light corn syrup
1/3 c. dark corn syrup

2/3 c. margarine, melted
    and slightly cooled
1 t. vanilla extract
1/4 t. salt
8-inch pie crust

In a bowl, combine all ingredients except pie crust; mix well. Pour into unbaked crust. Bake at 350 degrees for one hour. Let cool completely before slicing. Makes 8 servings.

Ovens can vary, so set a kitchen timer when the pan goes into the oven. Check for doneness after the shortest baking time given...if a little more time is needed, be sure to watch closely.

Autumn Spice Streusel Cake

Ellie Levesque
Upland, CA

This is a family favorite. I make it in October because it has the flavors of fall. It's a hit with my Bible study group too!

18-1/4 oz. pkg. spice cake mix
1 sleeve graham crackers,
   crushed
3/4 c. brown sugar, packed

1/2 c. butter, melted
2 t. cinnamon
Garnish: powdered sugar

Prepare cake mix according to package directions; set aside batter. In a separate small bowl, mix graham cracker crumbs, brown sugar, butter and cinnamon; set aside. Lightly coat a 12-cup Bundt® pan with non-stick vegetable spray. Pour half of batter into pan. Add all of crumb mixture; pour remaining batter on top. Bake at 350 degrees for 35 to 40 minutes, until cake tests done with a toothpick. Let cool. Turn out cake onto a cake plate; dust with powdered sugar. Serves 8 to 10.

One cool crisp fall day, my dad asked me to bring the grandchildren to the farm to pick apples. The apples were very small, but just right to can for pies and cobblers. Well, I talked a friend into helping me and we peeled our hearts out. The apples were so small by the time you peeled them, they were the size of a small egg! But they were free and we had a good time together. We made the best-tasting apple pies, small ones that were more like pocket pies for our children's small hands. My children still remember how much fun they had that day at Grandpa Curly's farm.

–Sandy Perry, Bakersfield, CA

Caramel Apple Pie Dump Cake
MaryAlice Dobbert
King George, VA

This recipe takes about five minutes to put together! Great fall flavors and aromas will warm your kitchen.

2 21-oz. cans apple pie filling
1/4 c. caramel ice cream topping
18-1/2 oz. pkg. yellow cake mix

1/2 c. butter, melted
Garnish: whipped cream or
   vanilla ice cream

Spray a 13"x9" baking pan with non-stick vegetable spray. Add pie filling and caramel topping; swirl mixture with a quick stir. Sprinkle dry cake mix evenly over the top; drizzle with melted butter. Bake at 350 degrees for 30 to 35 minutes. Let cool. Garnish portions with whipped cream or ice cream. Makes 8 to 10 servings.

Cherry Fluff Pie
Kim Jasper
Lancaster, OH

I love this tasty recipe because it's so easy! It's great for when company pops in, or the kids tell you at the last minute that they need something to take to school.

21-oz. can cherry pie filling
8-oz. container frozen whipped
   topping, thawed

9-inch graham cracker crust

Gently mix together pie filling and whipped topping; spoon into crust. Cover and chill for about one hour. Serves 8.

Serve hot spiced coffee with sweet autumn treats. Simply add 3/4 teaspoon pumpkin pie spice to 1/2 cup ground coffee and brew as usual.

Apple Pie Cobbler

Mary Casasanta
Tracy, CA

I have an apple tree in my backyard, and one year I ended up with about 50 pounds of apples! When I found a cobbler recipe, I decided to make my own version using my apples.

1 c. self-rising flour
1-1/4 c. sugar, divided
1 c. milk
3/4 c. butter, melted and divided

6 Granny Smith apples, cored
   and chopped
1 t. cinnamon

In a bowl, mix together flour, one cup sugar, milk and 1/2 cup butter. Pour batter into a greased 11"x7" baking pan; set aside. Toss apples with cinnamon and remaining sugar. In a skillet over medium heat, sauté apples in remaining butter until tender; spoon over batter in pan. Sprinkle with Streusel Topping. Bake at 375 degrees for 40 minutes. Serves 8.

Streusel Topping:

1 c. long-cooking oats,
   uncooked
3/4 c. brown sugar, packed

1/2 c. self-rising flour
1/2 c. chopped pecans
1/2 c. butter, softened

Mix together all ingredients with a fork until crumbly.

For delicious apple pies and cakes, some of the best apple varieties are Granny Smith, Gala and Jonathan as well as old-timers like Rome Beauty, Northern Spy & Winesap. Ask at the orchard...the grower is sure to have tips for you!

S'mores Cobbler

Audra Vanhorn-Sorey
Columbia, NC

A unique twist on a family favorite...it's sure to be a hit!

5-oz. pkg. cook & serve
  chocolate pudding mix
1 c. whole milk
6 whole graham crackers,
  broken in half
1/2 c. mini semi-sweet chocolate
  chips

18-1/2 oz. pkg. chocolate cake
  mix
1/2 c. butter, sliced
10-oz. pkg. marshmallows

Prepare pudding mix with milk according to package directions;
cool slightly. Spoon pudding into an ungreased 13"x9" baking pan.
Arrange graham crackers over pudding, with some space between
crackers. Sprinkle with chocolate chips; spread dry cake mix over top
and dot with butter. Bake at 350 degrees for 25 minutes. Remove
from oven; stir slightly to ensure all ingredients are moistened. Top
with marshmallows. Bake for an additional 8 to 10 minutes, until
marshmallows are melted. Makes 10 servings.

One of the best ways to give thanks is to help someone else.
Volunteer, lend a neighbor a hand, leave a surprise on someone's
doorstep...there are lots of thoughtful ways to show you care.

Desserts

IN A DASH

Tina's Marshmallow Pie

Tina Goodpasture
Meadowview, VA

I love mallow cups and think of them whenever I serve this creamy pie!

10-oz. pkg. mini marshmallows
1/2 c. milk
1/4 c. butter, sliced
1 c. frozen whipped topping,
    thawed

9-inch graham cracker crust
Garnish: chopped chocolate
    pieces or chocolate syrup

In a saucepan over low heat, combine marshmallows, milk and butter. Cook and stir until marshmallows are melted. Let cool; stir in whipped topping. Spoon into pie crust. Cover and chill. Garnish with chocolate pieces or drizzle with chocolate syrup, as desired. Makes 8 servings.

A quick & easy harvest decoration for cupcakes!
Flatten red, yellow and orange fruit roll-ups and cut with
a leaf-shaped cookie cutter, then press the "leaves"
onto frosted cupcakes.

Creamy Maple Rice Pudding

Andrea Heyart
Savannah, TX

*Creamy rice pudding flavored with real maple syrup and
brown sugar...pure comfort!*

3/4 c. water
3/4 c. instant rice, uncooked
2-3/4 c. whole milk
1 egg, beaten
1/3 c. maple syrup

1/3 c. brown sugar, packed
1 T. butter
1/2 t. cinnamon
Optional: 1/8 t. salt

Bring water to a boil in a large saucepan over medium-high heat. Stir
in rice. Remove from heat; cover and let stand for 10 minutes, or until
most of water is absorbed and rice is tender. Add milk to rice in
saucepan and return to a low boil, stirring occasionally. In a small
bowl, beat together egg, maple syrup and brown sugar. Slowly add
2 tablespoons of warm rice mixture to egg mixture; stir and add all
of mixture to saucepan. Stir in butter, cinnamon and salt, if desired.
Simmer over low heat, stirring constantly, for another 10 minutes, or
until thickened. Serve warm, or cover and refrigerate until chilled.
Makes 4 to 6 servings.

Press whole cloves into the surface of a pillar candle to form
a pattern...just right for a dessert buffet.

212

Butterscotch Chocolate Pudding

Shala Kerrigan
Anchorage, AK

My family loves pudding! They like the packaged kind, but they love it when I make pudding from scratch. My kids are 16 and 20 now, and they still run to the kitchen looking for the bowls and whisk to "clean" for me.

1/2 c. semi-sweet chocolate
   chips
1/4 c. butterscotch chips
1 egg, lightly beaten
2 c. milk
1/4 c. brown sugar, packed

1/4 c. baking cocoa
2 T. cornstarch
1 t. vanilla extract
1/8 t. salt
Garnish: whipped cream

Place chocolate and butterscotch chips in a large heatproof bowl; add egg and set aside. In a large saucepan, combine remaining ingredients except garnish; whisk well. Cook over medium heat, whisking constantly, until thickened. Pour hot milk mixture over chocolate chip mixture. Stir constantly until well combined and chips are melted. Spoon pudding into individual dessert bowls; cover and chill. Serve topped with whipped cream. Serves 6.

Before displaying gourds and pumpkins as a centerpiece, a quick wash will help them last longer. Stir together a tablespoon of bleach in a gallon of water, then gently wash and pat dry.

Pumpkin-Chocolate Chip Muffins

Carrie Kelderman
Pella, IA

Most of us cook with pumpkin only in autumn, but these muffins are a welcome treat any time of year. Our family loves them!

1 c. canned pumpkin
1/2 c. brown sugar, packed
1/4 c. butter, melted and slightly
    cooled
2 eggs, beaten

2 c. all-purpose flour
2 t. baking powder
1/2 t. salt
1 c. semi-sweet chocolate chips

In a large bowl, mix all ingredients in the order given. Spoon batter into paper-lined muffin cups, filling about 3/4 full. Bake at 375 degrees for 20 minutes, or until muffins test done with a toothpick. Makes one dozen.

Honey Cups

Jill Nikunen
Kalispell, MT

Several years ago I received this recipe from a patient where I worked. It is so easy and tasty! Perfect for school snacks, hiking trips or anytime. I almost always have to share the recipe!

3 c. long-cooking oats,
    uncooked
2 c. sweetened flaked coconut
1 c. whole-wheat flour, or
    1-1/3 c. all-purpose flour

2 c. chopped almonds
1 c. butter, sliced
1/2 c. honey
1 c. brown sugar, packed
1 t. vanilla extract

In a large bowl, combine oats, coconut, flour and almonds; set aside. In a saucepan over medium-low heat, combine butter, honey, brown sugar and vanilla. Bring to a boil; boil for one minute. Pour over oat mixture; mix well. Spoon batter into greased mini muffin cups, filling about 3/4 full. Bake at 350 degrees for 8 to 10 minutes, until golden. Cool muffins in tin for 5 minutes; remove to a wire rack. Makes about 4 dozen.

IN A DASH

Cotton Candy Muffins

Brenda Huey
Geneva, IN

*I came up with this recipe after we went to a county fair.
I love cotton candy and thought this combination would make
a wonderful muffin...it sure did!*

2 c. sugar	1 t. salt
1 c. margarine, softened	1 t. baking soda
1-1/2 c. sour cream	4 c. all-purpose flour
4 eggs, beaten	3 T. nonpareil sprinkles
1/2 c. maraschino cherry juice	Garnish: additional sprinkles

In a large bowl, combine sugar, margarine, sour cream and eggs. Add cherry juice, salt, baking soda and flour. Beat until well combined; stir in sprinkles. Pour into paper-lined muffin cups, filling 3/4 full. Bake at 325 degrees for 10 to 12 minutes, until muffins test done with a toothpick. Cool; frost with Buttercream Icing and top with a few extra sprinkles. Makes 1-1/2 dozen.

Buttercream Icing:

1/2 c. butter, softened	2 t. vanilla extract
4 c. powdered sugar	Optional: red or blue food
1/2 c. milk	coloring

In a large bowl, combine butter, powdered sugar and milk. Beat with an electric mixer on medium speed until smooth; beat in vanilla. If too thin, add more sugar. If desired, tint pink or blue with a few drops of food coloring to look like cotton candy.

When taking along snacks for the ride, slice cupcakes in half, frost and put them back together so that the frosting is in the middle...neat and tidy.

Potato Doughnuts

Nancy Diem
East Earl, PA

My mother-in-law gave me this recipe many years ago.
Very good. The doughnut holes are my favorite!

2 c. sugar
4 c. all-purpose flour
4 t. baking powder
1/2 t. salt
1 c. whole milk
1 c. cold mashed potatoes

1 T. butter, softened
3 eggs, beaten
oil for deep frying
Garnish: powdered sugar or
    cinnamon-sugar

In a large bowl, mix together sugar, flour, baking powder and salt.
Add milk, potatoes, butter and eggs; mix thoroughly. Roll out dough
on a well floured surface, about 3/4-inch thick. Cut out doughnuts
and holes with a doughnut cutter; set aside. Add 4 inches oil to a
large heavy saucepan. Heat to medium-high, about 360 degrees on a
candy thermometer. Carefully add doughnuts to oil, 2 to 3 at a time.
Cook, turning over, until golden on all sides. Cook doughnut holes the
same way. Drain well on paper towels. Sprinkle with powdered sugar
or cinnamon-sugar while still warm. Makes about 3 dozen.

It's the perfect time of year to share some tasty treats with
teachers, librarians and school bus drivers...let them know
how much you appreciate them!

IN A DASH

Amber's Cinnamon Bread

*Denise Webb
Newington, GA*

*This recipe was always my daughter's favorite quick bread.
Now as a mommy, she loves to make it for her kids.*

1 egg, beaten
1/4 c. oil
1-1/2 c. sugar, divided
2 c. all-purpose flour

1/2 t. salt
1 t. baking soda
1 c. buttermilk
1 T. cinnamon

In a large bowl, beat together egg, oil and one cup sugar; set aside. In a separate bowl, mix together flour, salt and baking soda. Add flour mixture to egg mixture alternately with buttermilk, stirring well. Combine cinnamon and remaining sugar in a cup. Spoon half of batter into a greased 9"x5" loaf pan; sprinkle with half of cinnamon-sugar. Repeat layers; swirl with a knife. Bake at 350 degrees for one hour. Cool for 10 minutes; turn out of pan. Makes one loaf.

For the tenderest quick breads and muffins,
don't overmix...just stir the batter until moistened.
A few lumps won't matter.

217

Index

Index

Index

Find Gooseberry Patch
wherever you are!

www.gooseberrypatch.com

Call us toll-free at 1·800·854·6673

homecoming parades · colorful leaves

casual get-togethers

drives in the country

craft fairs

moonlit hayrides

crackling bonfires · community suppers

U.S. to Metric Recipe Equivalents

Volume Measurements

1/4 teaspoon	1 mL
1/2 teaspoon	2 mL
1 teaspoon	5 mL
1 tablespoon = 3 teaspoons	15 mL
2 tablespoons = 1 fluid ounce	30 mL
1/4 cup	60 mL
1/3 cup	75 mL
1/2 cup = 4 fluid ounces	125 mL
1 cup = 8 fluid ounces	250 mL
2 cups = 1 pint =16 fluid ounces	500 mL
4 cups = 1 quart	1 L

Weights

1 ounce	30 g
4 ounces	120 g
8 ounces	225 g
16 ounces = 1 pound	450 g

Oven Temperatures

300° F	150° C
325° F	160° C
350° F	180° C
375° F	190° C
400° F	200° C
450° F	230° C

Baking Pan Sizes

Square	
8x8x2 inches	2 L = 20x20x5 cm
9x9x2 inches	2.5 L = 23x23x5 cm
Rectangular	
13x9x2 inches	3.5 L = 33x23x5 cm

Loaf	
9x5x3 inches	2 L = 23x13x7 cm
Round	
8x1-1/2 inches	1.2 L = 20x4 cm
9x1-1/2 inches	1.5 L = 23x4 cm